My Food Addiction Recov

2 … Welcome to Your Recovery from Food Addiction!

5 … Understanding Food Addiction

12 … Recovering Your Brain

29 … Identifying and Managing Triggers

43 … Surviving Withdrawals

50 … Defining Your Sobriety

60 … Developing a Healthy Relationship with Food

67 … Additional Tips for a Successful Recovery

82 … Next Steps

83 … Addendum

Welcome to Your Recovery from Food Addiction!

She stayed home from her high school reunion, too embarrassed because she had not lost her pregnancy weight and was still gaining… He felt humiliated on the plane when he realized his larger frame was taking up part of the seat of the woman next to him… She lost the weight before and put it on again; she just can't seem to keep it off… He thinks about food all the time and is planning the next meal before this one is even finished... She was passed over for a promotion that she was more qualified for than the less-experienced slender co-worker to whom it was given – and this isn't the first time this has happened. "They don't want a fat person to represent the company to the public," she tells herself… He hates using a C-PAP machine, but his snoring from his sleep apnea is so loud it keeps his wife awake. He didn't have that problem when he weighed less… Her glucose levels are in the pre-diabetic range but she just can't stop eating sugar even though it zaps her energy, she never feels well and has headaches… He had weight-loss surgery and successfully lost 80 pounds; since then, he has regained back 60 of those pounds. He despairs and wonders if he will ever be healthy… She longs to play on the floor with her grandchildren like their other grandmother does, but it is too difficult, and it's embarrassing to ask for help to get up… It's Friday night, and her roommates have all gone out. She is in the apartment with a bag of chips and a soda, alone again. "No one will ever want to go out with me – I am so fat."

The stories are heart-wrenching.

Perhaps you have faced some of the same experiences as the individuals above. Maybe you have also wondered why you can't lose weight or stay on a diet or stay off processed sugar. Maybe you have wondered about the possible addictive nature of your struggle with food.

Recent neuro-science research shows that activities such as over-eating – or the consuming of high-fat, high-sugar, high-salt (highly-palatable: desirable) foods – produces dopamine, a "feel-good" neurotransmitter released into the prefrontal cortex of the brain. This part of the brain is responsible for willpower, and when it's compromised due to repeated floods of dopamine, it can become addicted – just like that of a drug addict. It's as if the brain gets hijacked, so the next time you feel stressed, bored, lonely or upset, your brain says, "Hey, I know what to do with that! Pass the chips!"

Consider this definition of food addiction and see if it fits for you:

"Addiction is the use of a substance (like sugar) or an activity (like over-eating) to numb or change the way you feel that now cannot be stopped, even at the risk of your health and the quality of your life."

Take a minute to take the following quiz:

Is My Struggle with Food an Addiction?

1. Do you feel uncomfortable, embarrassed, guilty, or depressed about your physical appearance, your weight, or your eating habits?

2. Have you ever felt powerless to achieve a healthy weight because you have been unsuccessful in your previous attempts to lose weight permanently?

3. Do you resort to compulsive or emotional eating to escape from problems, avoid boredom, relieve anxiety, or cope with stress?

4. Have you ever tried to stop or limit some aspect of your compulsive-eating behaviors, but failed in your attempts?

5. Have you ever said, "This is the last time I will do that!" yet have continued to do it repeatedly in spite of the potential consequences?

6. Do you ever find yourself preoccupied or obsessed with thoughts about eating or about food? Is it a struggle to stop thinking about food?

7. Have your eating behaviors resulted in physical complications (such as pre-diabetes or diabetes, heart disease, high blood pressure, high cholesterol, or other potentially life-threatening diseases)?

8. Has someone close to you ever expressed concern about your weight or eating?

If you answered yes to any of the above questions, it may be an indication that you are addicted to eating or to specific highly-palatable foods.

When are we going to stop trying to treat addiction with a diet?

Right now! Welcome to the first step of your recovery from food addiction! <u>This is the secret, the missing piece – Diets don't treat addiction!</u> This workbook is designed to help you develop a plan for recovery, based on the research and experience of working with others who, like yourself, have an addiction to food. You can use this workbook alone, with a group of friends or with a therapist.

At times, you have probably been very committed to making healthy changes: a new diet, an exercise plan, a commitment to accept yourself as you are. Like every other person who has struggled with an addictive relationship with food, you have experienced times of success followed by setbacks and failures. With each

> Q. I have tried EVERYTHING! Why would I think this could work?
>
> A. You have tried a lot of things to change your relationship with food; diets, exercise, surgery. You haven't tried treating the addiction. This is the missing piece.

set back or failed attempt, you may have felt a confirmation of what you already believe deep within yourself – that life without compulsive eating is impossible. You likely hear inside yourself the words: "I can't do this." That belief comes from a place inside and can make a new commitment feel out of reach.

I am asking you to make a commitment from a different place inside you. You know it is there, or you would not be reading this workbook right now. It is a place of hope, a place of "maybe I can," or of "there has to be a better way." Let this part of you answer the call of recovery from food addiction.

While many individuals may need additional help, resources and support, this workbook is a great first step. Because support is so important, I encourage you to do this with a supportive friend or group of friends or with a therapist. Adding on a 12-Step meeting for food addiction is another powerful support you can use as you move through this workbook. At a 12-Step meeting you can request a sponsor who may be willing to help you work thru this book as well.

Now, you are on a path that can lead you to joy, confidence and freedom from food addiction.

JOURNAL ENTRY

To get you started, each section of this workbook provides space for you to journal. **Be sure to take the time to do this.** Use your *My Food Addiction Recovery Journal* for recording your progress and your thoughts as well. Use this section to write down some of the thoughts and feelings you are having, both negative and positive, as you embark on your path to recover from food addiction.

_____

_____

_____

_____

_____

_____

_____

_____

> **TOOL:** Journaling is a mindfulness activity and mindfulness helps the brain to heal from addiction!

Understanding Food Addiction

You've heard the term "comfort food." When you feel stressed, lonely, sad, anxious, or bored and you eat, you feel better, right? There are both biological reasons and emotional reasons for finding comfort in food. Let's take a look at each of these individually and see how they relate to food addiction.

Neurobiology of food addiction

First, it is important to understand what happens in our brain when we turn to food for comfort.

When we eat a food that brings us pleasure, like Grandma's apple pie, the brain releases dopamine which increases the desire (or amplifies the craving) for more of what gave us that pleasure. Dopamine doesn't create the pleasure from the apple pie, but it enhances our anticipation of pleasure. That is why when you are eating Grandma's apple pie, you are already thinking about having a second slice! That is why even when there is no pie, just thinking about it and remembering how pleasurable it was leads you to want to go and get some.

While some dopamine is good (and even essential) for optimal brain functioning, when we over-eat, binge, or eat compulsively we release more dopamine than is needed. This "feel-good" neurotransmitter is linked to the pleasure and reward system in the brain. It helps us numb out or de-stress. As we mentioned in the introduction, it is as if the brain has been hijacked, so now when we feel stressed, lonely, sad, anxious, or bored, our brain says, "Hey! I know what to do with that!" and we become fixated on food. Dopamine creates "pleasure pathways" in the brain. This is the process that is found in all addictions, including drug or alcohol addiction! Although we produce this neurotransmitter ourselves, if we repeatedly turn to this pleasure and reward system to manage our emotions, we run the risk of becoming addicted. MRI and SPECT scans show that the brain of a person bingeing and eating highly-palatable foods looks the same as the brain of a cocaine addict! So, you aren't actually addicted to eating – you are addicted to dopamine.[1] [2]

> Watch out for Addiction Transfer!
>
> Compulsive eating isn't the only dopamine-producing activity. Phone and video games, Internet activity, porn, social media, gambling and shopping can all produce dopamine as well. Remember your problem isn't with food, it's with dopamine; so limit or cease the above activities and let your brain heal!

Addictive foods

Another part of food addiction is the compulsive craving for highly-palatable foods. What are these foods? These are foods that are high in unhealthy fats, sugars, and salt. Typically, they are known as "junk foods," or processed foods. The Yale Food Addiction Scale identifies some of these as pizza, chocolate, cookies, chips, ice cream, French fries, cheeseburgers, sweetened sodas, cake, cheese, bacon, and fried chicken.[3] Studies show that many of these foods are engineered in a way to make them more "rewarding" to us than healthy foods, such as nuts, vegetables, seeds, and fruit. Many of them are infused with increased levels of unhealthy fats, sugar, food additives, and flavors. Junk foods stimulate the reward system in the brain the same way that drugs do in drug addiction. Eating a steady diet of "junk foods" can cause the same biological reaction as an addiction to abusive drugs, like cocaine.[4]

Willpower

So why isn't willpower enough to stop overeating, or eating unhealthy, addictive foods? Seventy percent of Americans are overweight in our country and unable to consistently maintain a healthy nutritional plan[5]. As Americans, we are an industrious, determined, highly-productive people. If this was only about willpower, we would have found the answer already.

---

[1] Gearhardt, A.,Yokum, S., Orr, P., Stice, E., Corbin, W. & Brownell, K., (2011). Neural correlates of food addiction. *Arch Gen Psychiatry.* 68(8):808-816.

[2] Blum, K., Chen, A., Giordano, J, Borestn, M., Chen, T. Hauser, M., Simpatico, T.,Femino, J., Braverman, E., Brah, D., (2012). The Addictive Brain: All Roads Lead to Dopamine, *Journal of Psychoactive Drugs*, 44 (2), 134–143, 2012

[3] Gearhardt, N., Corbin, W., & Brownell, K., (2009). Yale University, 2 Hillhouse Ave., New Haven, CT 06520.

[4] Blumenthal, D. & Gold, M., (2010). Neurobiology of food addiction. Current Opinion in Clinical Nutrition and Metabolic Care, 13:359–365

[5] Thacker, S., (2017). Food addiction, looking at binge-eating through a process-addiction lens. The Therapist. Jan-Feb, www.camft.org.

The prefrontal cortex is responsible for executive functioning, which includes judgement, decision making, follow through on goals, and for impulse control. This important part of our brain is also where our willpower lives.[6] So when a food addict floods their brain with dopamine repeatedly, willpower is compromised and diminished. The one thing they can't do is say no to food.

Of course, there is much more to how neurotransmitters and hormones work together and are compromised in food addiction, but this gives you a basic idea of what is happening. Knowledge is power, and when you understand something, you increase your power to manage it differently. Remember, you can't change what you can't see.

> Compulsion is compulsion is compulsion. Your brain cannot tell the difference between Compulsive Eating and Compulsive Dieting. It registers both as an addiction.

The Food Addiction Cycle

Understanding the Food Addiction Cycle will help you to develop new tools for stopping the cycle of compulsive eating.

Patrick J. Carnes, a nationally known speaker and author of several books on addiction and recovery, has identified four stages in the addiction cycle. That cycle has been adapted for food addiction below:

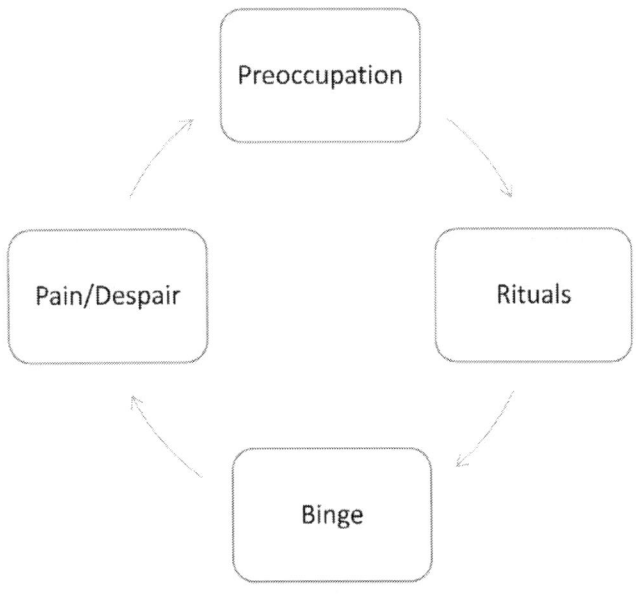

The Food Addiction Cycle

---

[6] Thacker, S., (2017). Food addiction, looking at binge-eating through a process-addiction lens. The Therapist. Jan-Feb, www.camft.org.

The cycle begins with some type of emotional pain or stress. It might be a feeling of rejection, anxiety, loneliness, depression, frustration, boredom or grief. It might come from feelings of failure or guilt, which may have been triggered by interpersonal conflict, another binge or even just tiredness. When we don't want to feel these emotions, we do something to distract ourselves from them. For food addicts, that distraction usually involves a dopamine-producing activity. like eating or binging on a highly-palatable or well-liked food.

However, it's not the pain that is the problem – it's running from the pain that's the problem! Learning to recognize the cycle in your own life can give you power to stop running from emotional or physical pain and learn healthier ways of managing your emotions.

Let's look at the Four Stages of the Food Addiction Cycle:

Preoccupation

Preoccupation is characterized by an obsessive or significantly intense focus on food and eating. This preoccupation is often used to mask or cover up pain of some sort, whether it is emotional or physical. Obsessing about food may even be used to escape the shame or guilt felt from a previous bingeing episode. No matter how satisfying or disappointing the last eating activity was, the addict frequently becomes preoccupied with seeking out food again in an attempt to feel better.

Rituals

Moving from preoccupation, the addict takes steps to get closer to the eating activity. These steps often take the form of rituals which may be so simple that the addict performs them almost unconsciously. This stage may include taking steps to eat in secret, purchase food alone, hide it for later, prepare it under the guise of it being for someone else, or finding ways to acquire food without the knowledge of others. For some, just finding coins to purchase a snack or searching out where to get the snack can be part of the ritual, which takes them one step closer to "acting out" with food. Addicts will often be angry or bothered when their rituals are disrupted or pointed out by someone else.

Binge

> Compulsion cannot coexist"
> - Geneen Roth

The Binge, which is what the first two steps have been driving toward, can also be called the Moment of Ecstasy. Acting out with food can be carried out on many different levels – from completely private, alone, and secretive, to eating with family or as a social activity with others. Another form of bingeing is "grazing", eating smaller amounts throughout a day thus unconsciously consuming larger amounts of calories than needed.

Pain / Despair The moment of ecstasy is often followed by a period of Pain/Distress. The pain may be the result of shame or guilt for having over-eaten or eaten unhealthy "taboo" foods. Self-loathing is the most common emotional response to a binge. There is likely physical discomfort as well such as bloating, painful fullness, flatulence, abdominal tension, or indigestion. Self-loathing is often the trigger to begin the cycle again.

An Illustration of the Addiction Cycle

PREOCCUPATION: Sara, a college student, finds herself thinking about how good it would be to get a cheeseburger and fries. She thinks about the different places she has eaten before. She thinks about what might taste good with the cheeseburger and fries, like a soda, or perhaps a milkshake. She is sure this will help her battle the stress of homework deadlines and exams, or maybe she even feels like this is a great reward for her hard work and studying.

RITUALIZATION: She stops at three different fast food establishments to acquire the specific foods she is craving, so no one will know how much she is really planning to eat. She orders as though the food is for herself and a friend, ordering two of each item. She pulls into a parking lot of a nearby park to eat her food so that her roommates won't know how much she is eating or see the wrappers. She carefully disposes of the "evidence."

BINGE: As she eats the food, she begins to feel comforted from the stress of the difficult classes she has been juggling. She feels a sense of calm, and a pleasurable sensation comes from the tastiness and flavor of the food. She feels temporarily happy, content, and free from the discomforts and pressures of school and her studies.

PAIN/DESPAIR: As she is finishing her food, she begins to feel out of control and disgusted by her actions. The pain gives way to shame and self-loathing thoughts. She vows never to eat this way again, then berates herself knowing that she will because this is a cycle that has repeated itself many times. She begins to feel bloated, uncomfortable, and experiences familiar indigestion from the food.

PREOCCUPATION begins again: Unable to tolerate the feelings of self-loathing, guilt, and lack of willpower, Sara shifts her focus to what she will eat at her next meal. She thinks about stopping at the store on the way home from school and buying some of her favorite candy to eat later tonight when she is done studying and can watch television and numb out.

TOOL: Tune In to YOU

Tuning in to you is a mindfulness exercise.

"What am I feeling?" This is an important question to ask yourself every day and all throughout the day. Once you know what you are really feeling, you can better understand what you really need and can take care of yourself in healthy ways. Tuning in to you takes practice, but once you learn to connect with your feelings and better understand your needs, you will know more about yourself and how to properly take care of YOU!

When feeling the need, desire, or compulsion to eat, "Tune In to YOU" first by asking the following questions:

What am I feeling physically?

What am I feeling emotionally?

What am I feeling spiritually?

Am I physically hungry? Or am I turning to food to cope with something?

If I am turning to food to cope, what triggered me?

What do I really need?

Once you recognize and accept what you are feeling inside, then you can make decisions about healthier ways to fill your need. For example, if you feel tired, sleep; if you feel lonely, call a friend; if you feel bored, find something to do that you enjoy; if you feel stressed, take some deep breaths and regroup, or participate in healthier and more fulfilling activities that bring relief. If physical hunger is what you feel, then take care of that need in a healthy way. If it is not really hunger you are "feeding," take care of the true need. One way to do this is to read a daily affirmation from your *My Food Addiction Recovery Journal* and work on your Dailies. I'll talk more about those in just a moment; first, let's do some journaling.

JOURNAL ENTRY

Use this section to write down some of the thoughts and feelings you are having as you learn more about food and eating as an addiction. How is this information helping you to understand why you have responded the way you have when it comes to eating and using food for more than just "fuel for the body?"

Recovering Your Brain

Now that you have a better understanding about the neurobiology of addiction and the addiction cycle, let's talk about what promotes healing and what you can do to create new neural pathways for a healthier, non-addicted brain.

Neuroscience has shown exciting recent advances in this area. We see that with practice and consistent participation in healthy daily activities, neural pathways can form new connections and strengthen those that are lacking. This also helps to speed transmission of information; in other words, it helps improve brain functioning![7]

> **Recovery is not a once a week process, Recovery is a "Daily" Action.**
>
> You've paid a lot of attention to your addictive behaviors. Equal focus needs to be given to your recovery. (You wouldn't sleep once a week and expect a productive outcome!) Make your Recovery a "Daily" Process.

The addicted brain can be positively affected by incorporating small, simple activities consistently into your daily routines. The following nine Cor-conditions of Recovery are categories from which you can choose daily activities that will help to move your brain functioning out of the instinctual limbic system and into the purpose-driven prefrontal cortex. This is why these are called "Cor"-conditions! What that really means for you is that there is a path which leads to removing the addict from the driver's seat of your life. You will be better able to take charge, use will-power, and make decisions to follow a healthier lifestyle.

Dailies

As you choose small, simple tasks called "Dailies" to do within the categories of the Nine Cor-conditions of Recovery each day, these "Dailies" will help you to stay focused on your recovery and to reprogram your brain. The Dailies may seem simplistic to you. You may be tempted at times to want to skip them. Remember that healing happens with *consistency* over *time*. Recovery is not a once a week process, but a "Daily" commitment to YOU! Don't skip your Dailies. If it feels overwhelming to you, then start with *just one thing* and build on that. Slowly you will find it easier to keep your focus and hold firm to your commitments. Your brain will experience healing and will grow new, healthier neural pathways.

> TIP: If you feel overwhelmed by the Dailies, make a mental shift in how you see them. This is not your To-Do List – this is your Self-Care List!

---

[7] Dweck, C., (2011). Decades of scientific research that started a growth mindset revolution. https://www.mindsetworks.com/science

Here are the Nine Cor-conditions for Recovery

1. Purposeful Activity
2. Mindfulness
3. A Healthy Relationship with Food
4. Connection
5. Self-compassion
6. Movement
7. Play
8. Music
9. Acts of Service

Let's get started!

Purposeful Activity

Addiction functions in the instinctual limbic system which influences impulse control. The ability to self-regulate is compromised, making it difficult to stay consistent with your goals to exercise or eat in healthy ways. You might also tend to procrastinate or avoid dealing with a problem today by rationalizing that you will take care of it tomorrow. This becomes problematic, keeping you from tasks and activities that are good for you. You may find it difficult to focus on what you need most and forget to take time for yourself for recreation and rejuvenation. Your ability to be patient with others might be affected and you may find that you are easily irritated with those around you. Re-training your brain to use its prefrontal cortex requires Purposeful Activities that can help you learn to self-regulate. Self-regulation refers to your ability to calm yourself when you're upset or make yourself feel better when you are down. Self-regulation also helps you to adapt to what is happening around you, make healthier food choices, and better manage eating. Self-regulate creates self-discipline which means you have better control of your own life.

Here are some ideas for Dailies to get you started in this area. Use the space below to brainstorm and list some ideas of your own:

wash-car
email-friend
take-a-class
frame-photo
read-book
recovery-reading
craft knit play-piano
learn-language
fold-laundry
paint cut-vegetables
fishing draw
gardening
workbook

More ideas:

___
___
___
___
___

Mindfulness

Like many people who struggle with food addiction, you may feel somewhat disconnected from your body. You may not recognize the signs and symptoms of hunger, sometimes termed "hunger denial". Often we confuse thirst and hunger and mistake one for the other. Sometimes we are just triggered by external sources like TV food commercials, driving past your favorite fast-food restaurant, magazine ads, smelling the familiar aromas of food. Stress if held in the gut may be mistaken for hunger. You might think these are hunger cues when it isn't. If you are disconnected from your body, you may also not recognize when you are full, which may lead you to continue eating mindlessly. You may not be aware of other needs that you have, either. You may use food to push down or suppress emotions in an attempt to avoid or not feel them.

> **Am I Hungry? Exercise**
>
> With one hand on your chest and one on your stomach, ask yourself, "Am I Hungry?" Notice where your hunger is. If it is in your stomach, it's time to eat something. If you feel it in your chest, it represents another hunger, not food hunger. Ask yourself, "What do I really need right now?" Rest? Connection? To do something you've been putting off?

As you become more mindful, you will begin to notice that you eat at times when you do not need food; you are not really hungry for "fuel." You may notice that you have emotions that need your attention. You will become more aware of you! More self-awareness means you will be more able to identify, address, and meet your real needs.

Mindfulness has also been shown to aid in healing the addicted brain and weight management[8,9]. Watch this short 5-minute video on Mindful Eating for more encouragement:
https://www.youtube.com/watch?v=sdmbEXEI6GA

Here are some ideas for Dailies in this area, to get you started. Use the space below to brainstorm and list some ideas of your own:

---

[8] Caldwell, Karen L; Baime, Michael J; Wolever, Ruth Q. (2011). Mindfulness Based Approaches to Obesity and Weight Loss Maintenance, *Journal of Mental Health Counseling;* Jul 2012; 34, 3.

[9] Garland, E. & Howard, M. (2018). Mindfulness-based treatment of addiction: current state of the field and envisioning the next wave of research, *Addiction Science & Clinical Practice;* **https://doi.org/10.1186/s13722-018-0115-3**

More ideas:

_____

_____

_____

_____

_____

A Healthy Relationship with Food

Nutrition is an important part of healing the brain from addiction. A healthy relationship with food includes abstinence from addictive and trigger foods. However, there are many other things that you can do to improve your relationship with food. As your brain is healing, you will become more consistent with living a healthy lifestyle with food. Reading the section on "Developing a Healthy Relationship with Food" in this workbook will give you some additional information and suggestions for this important Cor-condition. You may find it helpful to make an appointment with a registered dietitian* who is familiar with food addiction issues to help you make a solid and healthy routine[10]. Some of your Dailies will be surrounding making healthy choices, incorporating healthy foods in a balanced way. Other dailies will be more behavioral in nature and will focus on things like chewing well, slowing down, being more mindful as you eat, eliminating distractions and multitasking, etc. The *Just One Thing* document included in the Appendix

---

[10] * When working with a registered dietician, we recommend that you request that they use a Transtheoretical Model of Change which is consistent with the addiction cycle.

guides you in making just one change a week towards a healthier you. Check out the accompanying *Just One Thing Tracker to* help you track your progress.

Here are some ideas for Dailies to get you started:

honor-your-hunger
no-TV-while-eating
eat-every-few-hours   no-eating-after-7:00
chop-some-veggies-for-stir-fries-and-soups   no-soda
                                                    healthy-oils
eat-mindfully add-a-vegetable-to-my-meals see-the-dietician
write-my-food-plan-for-the-day Just-One-Thing   eat-for-fuel
minimum-9-cups-of-water
dark-leafy-greens

More ideas:

_____

_____

_____

_____

_____

Connection

Isolation is one of the most common – and most significant – stumbling blocks faced by individuals with food addiction. When you begin to feel rejection, anger, fear, or any strong emotion, a natural response is to retreat or lash out as a means of pushing away. Whether you retreat or lash out, you create aloneness. It often seems easier to be alone and to isolate from others than to reach out for support. There is often a strong sense of embarrassment or shame involved that stems from a belief that something is wrong with us or that we are "damaged goods."

Research shows that healthy connections with others help to "rewire" the brain from addictive behaviors. This means that healing can occur when we strengthen our personal relationships. When we connect with others, we release oxytocin, an important hormone that plays a major role in attachment. Attachment is a primary need for all human beings. Unlike the excitement of dopamine (found in food addiction), oxytocin "produces feelings of deep affection, serenity and the desire for cooperation"[11], [12].

Many people who struggle with food addiction feel embarrassed and may dismiss the suggestion to connect with others because of the discomfort they feel. Perhaps it is scary to be vulnerable with another person and put your imperfections out there. You may not trust that others will be there for you. Maybe you are afraid of judgment or rejection. You might say, "I don't need anyone else's help. I can do it myself." **Remember, if you could do this yourself, you would have done it already.**

Start setting up your support system. Talk about your food addiction with others who can be there for you in your recovery. Identify those with whom you have a trusting relationship or with whom you can grow a closer relationship. You may also want to consider professional help and support if you feel your support system is inadequate. The "Circle of Support" exercise in the "Additional Tips" section of this workbook can help you identify or create a support system for yourself.

Here are some ideas for Dailies in the area of Connection to get you started. Use the space below to brainstorm and list some ideas of your own:

---

[11] Regier, M. W. (2011). Emotion-focused Couples Therapy, Valley Health Magazine.

[12] Wilkinson, L., Rowe, A., Bishop, R., Brunstrom, J., (2015). Attachment anxiety, disinhibited eating and body mass index in adulthood. *International Journal of Obesity*, 34, 1442–1445

More ideas:

_____

_____

_____

_____

_____

Self-Compassion

Self-loathing exists in everyone in varying degrees but it is particularly strong in the presence of addiction. In fact, it often precedes the addiction itself and it certainly reinforces it. This part of you often develops as a means to keep you in line or push you to follow the rules. It says things like, "You are pathetic! Look at you eating donuts again," trying to shame you into submission. It makes you feel unworthy of good things, and you stop reaching for them.

Self-compassion, on the other hand, is productive and carries the message, "I made a mistake. I can and will do it better." Self-loathing carries a message of shame and says, "I am the mistake" or "I never follow through." It shuts you down, undermines your self-confidence, and causes you to give up. Learning to recognize the persistent nature of your self-loathing voice can give you power to be more compassionate with yourself and achieve more productive results.

Of course, treating yourself with compassion doesn't mean saying, "I've had a rough day so I deserve cookies." Rather it says, "I've had a rough day. It's okay for me to have these feelings. I think I will go home and curl up with a good book and a cup of herbal tea this evening."

Here are some ideas for Dailies in the area of Self-Compassion to help get you started. Use the space below to brainstorm and list some ideas of your own:

Read-affirmations   read-about-self-compassion
Take-a-self-compassion-break
Journal make-a-gratitude-list
write-a-self-compassion-letter do-something-you-like-to-do
use-self-compassion-voice
talk-to-a-friend
reach-out

Note: The Self-Compassion Break can be found at **www.self-compassion.org/exercise-2-self-compassion-break**

More ideas:

_____

_____

_____

_____

Movement

Studies show that exercise can help return dopamine to normal levels[13]. If you have been sedentary, you needn't run out and engage in a strenuous fitness program – just start moving more. In his video titled "23½ hours[14]", Dr. Mike Evans lists the following benefits just from walking 150 minutes a week, which can even be broken down into 10-minute segments:

- Decreases the pain of knee arthritis by 47%
- Decreases progression to dementia by 50%
- In high risk patients, the progression to frank diabetes is lowered by 58%
- 23 % lower risk of death
- #1 treatment for fatigue
- Increased quality of life

Movement is healthy for the physical body; it promotes health and vitality. It also has numerous emotional benefits such as it can help you gather your thoughts, blow off some steam, and slow down the hurried pace of your day-to-day world.

Be sure to track you Movement Minutes in your *My Food Addiction Recovery Journal*.

Here are some ideas for your Movement Dailies to get you started. Use the space below to brainstorm and list some ideas of your own:

---

[13] Thacker, S., (2017). Food addiction, looking at binge-eating through a process-addiction lens. The Therapist. Jan-Feb, www.camft.org

[14] Evans, M., (2011), 23½ Hours, https://www.youtube.com/watch?v=aUaInS6HIGo&t=28s

wii-sports golf fly-a-kite walk my-fitness-pal yoga dance-DVD pedometer hike roll-office-chair-in-kitchen take-the-stairs fit-bit bike line-dance

More ideas:

_____

_____

_____

_____

_____

Play

As adults, we may neglect play. We get busy with work, responsibilities and the daily tasks of life. If you had a difficult childhood, it is possible that you never learned how to play. If you have always struggled with obesity, you may have felt too self-conscious to play or your size may have been limiting in terms of the activities you would feel comfortable participating in. Reclaiming our inner child through play is an important and necessary component in recovery and can help you experience a more joyful way of living. It may feel awkward at first, but if you keep at it you will come to love this part of your life.

Here are some ideas for Dailies in the area of Play to get you started. Use the space below to brainstorm and list some ideas of your own:

play-catch
squirt-guns
funny-movie
crafting
make-a-snowman bowling
attend-a-car-show fly-a-kite
art
Words-with-Friends line-dancing
water-balloons bubbles decorate-for-a-holiday
play-with-children attend-a-community-festival
miniature-golf
cards scrabble go-to-a-parade
board-games scrapbooks jacks
date-night
checkers

More ideas:

_____

_____

_____

_____

_____

23

Music

Music can make us feel happy. When we hear a song with a bouncy beat, it can be quite energizing. We hear a song about a lost love and it can make us feel sad. Music can bring up powerful emotions and memories. It might even take us right back to where we were when we heard that special song and our feelings were so intense. Music can help us to relax or make us want to get up and dance! There are times when the lyrics from a song can speak things to us internally that make a huge impact. Unlike the unhealthy altering of mood through over-eating, music's positive effects on the brain have been shown to aid in the recovery from addiction[15] [16]. Intentionally add some listening times into your recovery plan, like during your commute to and from work or while you are getting ready for the day you . Try some relaxing music at the end of the day to help you unwind! Check out the "Recovery Playlist" tip in the "Additional Tips for a Successful Recovery" section for more ideas.

Here are some ideas for Dailies with Music to get you started. Use the space below to brainstorm and list some ideas of your own:

COUNTRY   WORSHIP-MUSIC
PLAY-AN-INSTRUMENT ROMANTIC-MUSIC
ROCK-N-ROLL-TO-DANCE-TO
MAKE-MUSIC SING-ALONG-MUSIC-IN-THE-CAR
ENCOURAGING-MUSIC-WHILE-DRESSING
CARIBBEAN-MUSIC CALMING-MUSIC-AT-DINNER
CLASSICAL-MUSIC

---

[15] Blum, K., Chen, T., Chen, A., Madigan, M., Downs, W., Waite, R., Braverman, E., Kerner, M., Bowirrat, A., Giordano, J., Henshaw, H., Gold, M. (2010) Do dopaminergic gene polymorphisms affect mesolimbic reward activation of music listening response? Therapeutic impact on Reward Deficiency Syndrome (RDS). *Medical Hypotheses 74 (2010)* 513-520.

[16] Polston, J., Rubbinaccio, H., Morra, J., Sell, M., Glick, S., (2011). Music and methamphetamine: Conditioned cue-induced increases in locomotor activity and dopamine release in rats, *Pharmacology, Biochemistry and Behavior 98,* 54–61.

More ideas:

Acts of Service

Service has long been recognized in the Twelve Step world as an integral principle in recovery from addiction[17]. Helping someone else gives meaning to life and increases feelings of satisfaction. It helps you feel good about yourself.

Think about a time when you did something for someone else. How did you feel? What was their reaction? Simple Acts of Service bring us up and out of ourselves, uplifting our spirits as we reach out to others. It helps us balance our focus. Turning to others reinforces the positive impact of connection. It can also help to decrease stress and ease depression.

Here are some ideas for Dailies for Acts of Service to get you started. Use the space below to brainstorm and list some ideas of your own:

run-an-errand-for-a-friend
take-a-meal-to-a-sick-friend
send-an-encouragement-card
volunteer-at-soup-kitchen
bring-in-a-neighbor's-trash-can
pick-up-some-groceries-for-an-overwhelmed-friend
assemble-gift-bags-for-the-homeless
babysit-a-friends-kids
wash-the-car
encouraging-note-in-child's-lunchbox
text-an-affirmation-to-a-friend
post-it-note-for-spouse

More ideas:

_____

_____

_____

_____

_____

---

[17] Pagano, M., Krentzman, A., Onder, C., Baryak, J., Murphy, J., Zywiak, W., & Stout, R., (2010) Service to Others in Sobriety (SOS). *Alcohol Treat Q. 2010 April 1; 28(2):* 111–127.

Scoring your Dailies

- An important part of your recovery is structure and preparation. Your brain likes this! For this reason, Dailies must be planned in advance. This makes for intentional living. Plan your Dailies in the evening so that the next day you have already decided what you will do and you are prepared.

- Choose 7 Dailies from the Cor-conditions to do the following day and fill them out on the Cor-card in your My Transformation Journal*.

- You don't have to choose a Daily in every Cor-Condition category each day. Just try to cover each of the Cor-conditions sometime during the week.

- At the end of your day, check off the ones you completed and give yourself 1 point for each.

- There are 0-7 points possible each day and 0-49 points possible for the week.

- At the end of the week, tally all of your points. Participants who consistently score above 40 are usually working a good recovery program! This means that you can miss one Daily each day OR skip an entire day every week and still be working a good recovery. You don't have to be perfect to get better.

> Remember, purposefully doing the Dailies consistently over time is what will keep you in your recovery!

Remember, this is not your To-Do List. Think of it as your Self-Care List!

*The *My Food Addiction Recovery Journal* can be purchased separately. Please visit amazon.com/author/staceybthacker to order your journal.

JOURNAL ENTRY

Use this section to write down some of the thoughts and feelings you have had while working through this section. What obstacles do you see that might block you from doing your Dailies? How will you handle these obstacles?

Identifying and Managing Triggers

Triggers activate compulsive-eating thoughts and behaviors. Obvious triggers are **Food Triggers** such as specific foods, pictures of foods, food smells, conversations about food, food advertisements, or cooking shows on TV. Other triggers are **Location Triggers** such as passing by a favorite fast-food establishment, restaurant or grocery store. Then there are **Situational Triggers** such as common events, holidays, birthdays, special occasions, business meetings, vacations and other seasonal triggers.

There are other less obvious triggers that can be even more powerful than food, location, and situational triggers. These subtle triggers are **Emotional Triggers**: stress, boredom, frustration, anger, grief, rejection, loneliness, anxiety, fear, depression, etc. Positive emotions may also trigger cravings such as the excitement of going out with friends or a celebration. **Thought Triggers** are the thoughts that accompany the emotions you experience such as, "I am not good enough;" "No one will ever love me at this weight;" "Good things happen for other people but not for me;" or "I'm never going to get this right."

It is helpful to understand that in early in recovery, recognizing triggers often happens in retrospect, after a slip or relapse. These slips or relapses can be powerful learning opportunities. The more that you work on understanding your triggers, slips and relapses, the more you will increase in your ability to manage them better.

As you work through the following exercise, you may find yourself triggered but this exercise is helpful as it can "demystify" the triggers that have held power over you in the past. M. Scott Peck, author of *The Road Less Traveled* said that naming something gives you power over it. Naming the triggers that have had such a devastating effect on your life can start you on a journey of deeper understanding and eventually give you power over your triggers. When you recognize your triggers and have a plan for dealing with them, you can become empowered to use the tools in this workbook *before* the trigger strikes and weakens your resolve.

Take a few minutes to brainstorm and list as many triggers as you can. Then during this coming week simply notice your triggers and add these additions to the list:

_____

_____

_____

_____

You can use one of the Tips or Tools in this workbook or use your Dailies to manage your triggers. Changing from using food to incorporating other healthy and healing activities will help you begin to manage your triggers more effectively.

Identifying and Managing Triggers Exercise

My Food Triggers

Trigger foods ignite cravings, increase the desire for certain foods and may lead a food addict to lose control over their ability to manage what and how much they eat. Trigger foods often lead to episodes of binge eating, more mindless eating, or a continual over-consumption of food throughout the day sometimes referred to as "grazing." Identifying these trigger foods and making them less accessible is key to developing a healthy relationship with food.

TIP: How to recognize Trigger Foods

Remember the old Lay's potato chip slogan "Bet you can't eat just one!"? If you are eating ice cream, chips, or cookies and can't put them down when you are no longer hungry, then it's probably a trigger food. Additionally, there are some things that we eat that trigger a desire for other foods. For example, for some people, eating a cheeseburger can trigger the desire to have French fries and a milkshake. Be watchful about this and look for your Trigger Foods. Then identify the thing you can do (Tool) to lessen or eliminate their power over you.

Example:
Trigger:
"Chips are a trigger food for me. I can't eat a small amount; I eat the entire bag."

Tool:
I won't keep chips in my house.
(Cor-condition: Healthy Relationship with Food- Daily: Set up my environment for success)

What are some foods that you have difficulty putting down or that you can't stop eating once you start to eat them?

Circle your trigger foods:

      ice cream   chocolate   donuts   cookies   cake   candy

      white bread   rolls   pasta   chips   pretzels   crackers

      bacon   hamburgers   cheeseburgers   pizza   French fries

      diet soda   soda   other _____

TIP: Track some of your suspect foods this week and list the effects they have on you. For example, when you eat a taco, do you have to have a soda with it? When you eat chips, does it cause you to eat more of them or finish the bag? Do you get a headache or migraine from eating a certain food or eating too much of it? Do you feel bloated or gassy afterwards? These may be signs of trigger foods that you will need to avoid as part of your sobriety.

Trigger_____

_____

Tool_____

_____

Trigger_____

_____

Tool_____

_____

My Location Triggers

Example:
Trigger: *I get really triggered by seeing fast food restaurants, even if I just ate an hour ago. The car seems to drive itself into the drive thru. Before I know it, I am pulling out of the drive thru with a bag full of food!*

TOOL: I will use the "Am I Hungry?" Exercise and consciously decide to either eat or determine what I really need. This tool is found in the Understanding Food Addiction section.
(Cor-condition: Mindfulness- Daily: "Am I Hungry?" Exercise)

Trigger_____

_____

Tool_____

_____

Trigger_____

_____

Tool_____

_____

My Situational Triggers

Example:

Trigger: *I always bake cookies or make fudge for the neighbors at Christmas time. They will be expecting it! I really like doing this for them, but if I make these, I know I will eat them.*

Tool: *This year, I will put together Christmas baskets of a home-made potpourri for my neighbors with a note of gratitude for them being in our life. (Side Note: The weight-conscious neighbors love this!) (Cor-condition: Service- Daily: Do something for someone else)*

Trigger_____

_____

Tool_____

_____

Example (seasonal):

Trigger: *It's summer and there are so many barbecues. It's all about the food for me, and I especially have a hard time with the carbs: potato salad, chips and cookies.*

Tool: *I will be sure to take a seat away from the food table. I will offer to bring a healthy side dish. (Cor-condition: Healthy Relationship with Food- Daily: plan ahead). I will focus on my conversations with other people, listening more and asking them questions. (Cor-condition: Connection- Daily: Get to know someone)*

Trigger_____

Tool _____

_____

My Emotion Triggers – Food management or pain management?

It is important to note that recovery from food addiction is not about food management – it is about pain management. As you have read so far, food is used as a way to avoid feeling or as a way to numb ourselves from unpleasant or uncomfortable feelings. The addiction cycle is often initiated and maintained by faulty beliefs (thoughts) that you may have about yourself which influence how you perceive your reality. These beliefs determine the most important task in your life – how you make choices and decisions. For the addict, these beliefs tend to be shame-based and drive the addiction cycle.

4 Faulty Beliefs (thoughts):

1. My needs will never be met if I have to trust others to meet them (and so I meet them myself- with food).
2. I am not good enough to deserve good things in my life.
3. Life without compulsive eating (sugar, fast food, etc.) seems impossible.
4. No one would love me just as I am.

This diagram shows how these 4 Faulty Beliefs fit into the Addiction Cycle:

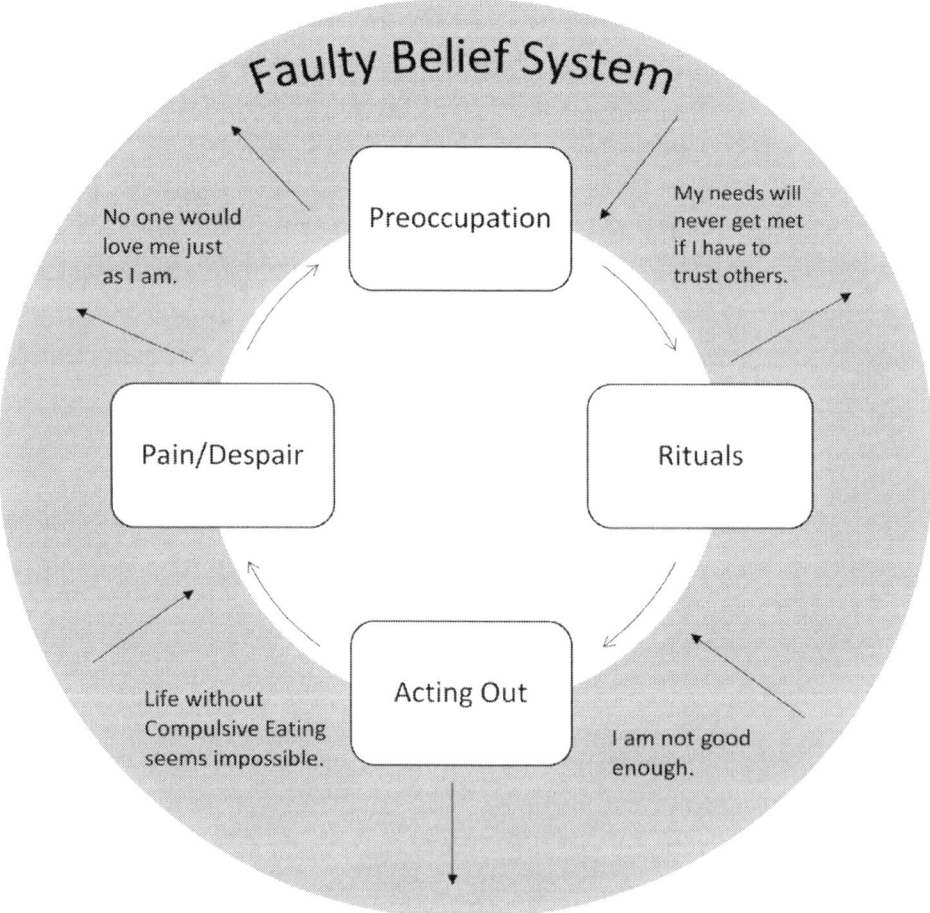

It is important for you to realize that these shame-based thoughts and beliefs are actually faulty and inaccurate, even though you may believe that they are true. It is quite likely that they are at the root of your addiction.

This faulty belief system may originate from experiences and pivotal events in your family growing up, your religious upbringing, your neighborhood, your elementary school, etc. If you a faulty belief system, these beliefs may have come from early childhood experiences, possibly in a dysfunctional family. Perhaps you had a perfectly acceptable childhood but developed a faulty belief system as an adult during difficult challenges or unhealthy relationships. It does not really matter how or where you picked up your faulty beliefs – what matters is that you are willing to face them and take the steps necessary to start down the path of recovery. **Some food addicts find that this is a good time to seek therapy to help sort out some of these feelings and thoughts.**

The Faulty Belief System fits into four specific areas of how we see ourselves, and how we relate to the world. These four areas are: Self-Image, Relationships, Needs and Compulsive Eating.

Self-Image
How do you perceive yourself? Most addicts compare themselves with other people. They see themselves as not being as good as others. They believe they are a failure; that they are undeserving, lacking will-power, or are weak and powerless to make permanent changes. When you act out with compulsive-eating behaviors and are unable to stop or control them, your faulty beliefs are confirmed. You may spend a considerable amount of time maintaining your image, overcompensating for your perceived deficiencies, or blaming others for your problems. Many addicts are perfectionists who play the exhausting game of overachievement due to the debilitating fear that they will be found out, judged, or that they will fail.

Relationships
Does your spouse or partner complain that you seem aloof, unavailable, distant, or disconnected in the relationship? A faulty belief system often contributes to the lack of connectedness in the addict's relationships. Since most addicts feel unlovable, they believe that no one could ever love them as they really are, so they must hide their real self and their addictive habits and patterns. The fear of being rejected by those closest to them can be so strong that the addict retreats into his/her own private world, sometimes a secretive world of compulsive or addictive eating.

Needs
Are you generally very independent, preferring to do things yourself rather than asking for help? Most addicts have trust issues and feel that they can depend on no one. It seems easier and safer not to rely on anybody else especially when it comes to having their needs met. Food addicts commonly feel that they can heal themselves. They want to believe that they do not need a therapist or one of "those groups." In their minds, they are certain that they can handle things on their own despite repeated failed attempts to control their eating patterns.

Compulsive Eating
Could you survive without compulsive eating? A compulsive eater's life becomes unmanageable when food is the most important thing in their life. Life without compulsive eating can seem terrifying or impossible, so the addict will work to maintain access to certain types and amounts of foods "just in case."

EXERCISE: Emotion Triggers: Four Faulty Core Beliefs (Thoughts)

This section will help you identify Emotion Triggers based on what you just learned about the Faulty Core Beliefs. Read each of the four Faulty Core Beliefs again and complete the accompanying sentences. <u>Please do not feel like you must limit your response to the space provided.</u> You will gain the most benefit from these exercises if you answer each question openly, honestly, and completely.

1. SELF-IMAGE:

"I am not good enough."

Example:
When I feel bad about myself, I cover up my feelings by being an exemplary employee or trying diet after diet to lose weight, as though 'looking better' will make me feel good about myself. Or, I shift the focus off myself by being highly critical of others, becoming an overachiever, distracting myself with food, etc.

I feel that I am not good enough when:

___

___

___

I cover up my true feelings about myself by:

___

___

___

I tend to feel best about myself when:

___

___

___

2. RELATIONSHIPS: (Note: Food addicts have often described that they confuse food with comfort or even love; they may even consider food a friend.)

"No one will love me just the way I am."

Examples:

If my partner knew how much I really eat, or that I hide food, they would be disgusted with me or they may judge me; therefore, I will never disclose the full extent of my compulsive-eating behaviors to them.

My family thinks I am so good and have it all together. I can't bear the thought of their disappointment in me. Eating makes me feel better.

In what ways are the above statements, or similar statements, true for you?

_____

_____

_____

_____

3. NEEDS:

"I can't trust others to meet my needs."

Examples:
I have to do everything myself to make sure things are done right or *I'm very independent and I rarely ask for help.*

I would rather do things myself because:

_____

_____

_____

_____

"It is not like me to ask for help." How does this statement apply to your life?

_____

How do you meet your own needs – for love, acceptance and belonging – with food?

> *"In the heat of my sugar addiction, I was not only hiding candy - I was hiding wrappers. When I began hiding wrappers in my children's soiled diapers so my spouse would not know how much candy I consumed, I realized the severity of my addiction."*
> -A recovering food addict

4. COMPULSIVE-EATING

"Life without compulsive eating seems impossible."

Examples:

I go to bed thinking about food, and I wake up thinking about food.
I can't concentrate or continue with my work until I eat.
If I am working on the computer, I think better with a bowl of snacks.
I can't relax or de-stress without eating.
I don't know how to have fun without food involved.
TV and popcorn go together; I have to have mine when I watch my favorite show.
I can't go to sleep unless I eat first; otherwise, I feel like something is missing.

What would happen in your life if you were unable to continue your compulsive-eating behaviors and patterns (which may include hiding food or fantasizing about food)? What would it be like to not comfort or show love through food? How would you comfort and express love without food?

___

My Emotion Triggers
Now you can identify some of your Emotion Triggers by working through this section.

Example:

Trigger: *Between work and the kids it feels like I am on the go all the time. I often feel overwhelmed! It's easier to just pick up fast food on the way home from soccer practice. (Faulty Belief: Life without fast food is impossible.)*

Tool: *I will wake up 20 minutes earlier on busy days so that I have time to plan and prepare food for the day. I will start dinner during this time: fix a salad, defrost some meat, and chop up some vegetables to cook. I can even put out the rice cooker with the rice already measured so I only have to add water and turn it on when we get home. (Cor-condition: "Healthy Relationship with Food" Daily -Prepare food ahead.)*

Trigger_____

Tool_____

Trigger_____

39

Tool _____

_____

Trigger: *I worry about how others see me and whether or not I am measuring up. This often leaves me feeling inadequate. This feeling comes to me most evenings when I get home. After work, I like to watch TV while I eat, but I have noticed that I eat until the show is over instead of stopping when I am full. (Faulty Beliefs: "I am not enough"; "No one will love me as I am.")*

Tool: *I used to love to knit and found it relaxing. I will take up knitting again and will knit a scarf while I watch TV (Cor-condition: "Purposeful Activity" Daily – knit.)*

Trigger _____

_____

Tool _____

_____

Trigger _____

_____

Tool _____

_____

Continue to add to your list of triggers and the tools for managing them. This is the work of recovery and will help you to take charge of your journey to sobriety.

Which One will You Feed? A TOOL for Managing the 4 Faulty Beliefs and Triggers

A legend, often attributed to the Cherokee, speaks of a grandfather who is teaching his grandson about life. He tells a story of two wolves who are fighting. "One," he says, "is angry, envious, and greedy. He lives with regret, arrogance, self-pity and pride. The other is kind, humble, compassionate, and full of empathy, generosity and faith."

The grandson asked, "But Grandfather, which one will win?"

The wise grandfather responded simply, "The one you feed."

There are two wolves inside us. One holds a Shame Voice; the other, a voice of Self-Compassion. The Shame Voice tells us lies, such as: "Why are you even trying to eat healthy? You know you are going to fail; you always do," "So what if you lost 5 pounds. You still have 100 to go!" and "Oh, you think you are doing so good to be getting out here and walking. See that runner over there? You'll never be able to do that."

The Self-Compassion Voice holds the truth. It says: "I have done hard things before – I can do this too." It points out your non-scale victories: "I ate vegetables at lunch!" "I walked 150 minutes last week!" and "I am strong in my recovery today."

A recovering food addict shared the following:
I was using food to numb the Shame Voice. At first, there was no Self-Compassion Voice – I didn't even have a script for this. But I found two things that helped me to develop my Self-Compassion Voice:

1. **Gratitude.** *If I walked up a flight of stairs and I was winded, my Shame Voice would jump in to berate me for being so fat and "out of shape." Because all I could see was my deficits, my Self-Compassion Voice sounded ridiculous at first, but I used it anyway. I said to myself, "I am grateful I have legs to walk up these stairs with and the more I do this the easier it will become for me." Over time, gratitude came more easily and my Self-Compassion Voice became louder.*

2. **Connection**. *Because food addiction lives in isolation, I forced myself to share the comments of my Shame Voice with one other person and with my food addiction recovery group. It was hard. I had to be vulnerable. Sometimes I had to let the others know what it was that I needed to hear back from them. As I did this, the Shame Voice got quieter. It wasn't so powerful when I shared it with others.*

Now my Self-Compassion Voice is stronger than my Shame Voice! When the Shame Voice activates, I can be curious about it, confront it, and replace it with statements of compassion and gratitude. Also, I can reach out to others which strengthens my connection with them."

Increase your awareness of your Shame Voice; recognize it and begin replacing it with statements your Self-Compassion Voice would say. No matter how foreign it sounds or feels at first, remember that over time it will become easier and it will grow to become the dominate voice in your thoughts.

Shame Voice or Self-Compassion Voice? Which one will you feed?

JOURNAL ENTRY

Use this section to write down some of the thoughts and feelings you experienced with the Identifying and Managing My Triggers exercise and with the story of the Two Wolves as it relates to you. How will listening to your Self-Compassion Voice help you overcome toxic shame and be successful in your recovery?

_____

_____

_____

_____

_____

_____

_____

_____

Surviving Withdrawal

While you are working on crucial Bottom Lines to stop bingeing or to not eat sugar or fast food, you may experience withdrawal. When faced with the uncomfortable symptoms of withdrawal, uninformed food addicts may experience setbacks in their recovery. Understanding withdrawal will help you proactively manage the symptoms successfully and continue to move forward in your recovery. "Be prepared" is good advice for all of us but it can have special significance for you at this point in your process. Let's discuss what you can expect and give you some tips and tools that will help you move through withdrawal and strengthen your recovery efforts.

I could understand withdrawal symptoms from drug or alcohol use, but I couldn't understand how quitting certain foods or stopping binge-eating could possibly have the same effect as withdrawal from drugs. Then my withdrawals started! I was irritable, had headaches, felt anxious and couldn't focus. A deep sadness set in, then anger. I worried that something was seriously wrong with me! Learning about withdrawal and its accompanying symptoms helped me to see that what I was experiencing was normal. I became open to using the tools I was learning about to help me deal more effectively with my withdrawals... and they did pass!

The above scenario is an illustration of what a recovering addict may think and experience when dealing with the issues of withdrawal from food addiction. In fact, when withdrawal symptoms begin to surface, it is a sign that you are truly in recovery.

Understanding Addiction and Withdrawal

When you repeatedly activate the pleasure pathways in your brain with the neurotransmitter dopamine and then stop, your brain goes into overdrive in an attempt to get you to keep those pathways open. It's as though your brain is screaming at you to eat! When this begins happening to you, it is a sign that you have entered the withdrawal stage.

During this stage, you may find yourself questioning whether you really have an addiction. You may say things like: *"I am not an addict. I can stop overeating any time I want. I have done it a hundred times"* or *"Other people can eat sugar, why can't I? I just need more will power."* You think: *"I can control this. I will just eat one cookie after dinner."* Of course this rarely works. You might find yourself holding the line for a day or two but as you've experienced in the past, you won't be able to sustain that.

Remember the definition of addiction we gave you earlier:
"Addiction is the use of a substance (like sugar) or an activity (like over-eating) to numb or change the way you feel that now cannot be stopped, even at the risk of your health and the quality of your life."
Although going through withdrawal can be a difficult struggle, there is life on the other side once you work through it. The sooner you face this, the sooner you will get to the other side. After you go through withdrawal, you will see that the intensity of the cravings begin to calm down and you will have more power

to manage your addiction. That can be a very exciting thing as you discover life on the others side of this addiction.

Symptoms of Withdrawal

Withdrawal symptoms generally last anywhere from two to 12 weeks with the first two to five days being the most difficult. While many recovering addicts will experience one or more of these symptoms, some do not have any. Each individual is different.

The most frequent symptoms experienced by recovering food addicts include:

- cravings
- headaches
- body aches
- cold sweats
- irritability
- anxiety
- mood swings
- insomnia
- fatigue
- shakiness
- sadness, loss

The following story illustrates the process of withdrawal and the victory of overcoming it.

In early recovery, I set my first Bottom Lines around not bingeing and not eating sugar. During the first week, I noticed I had difficulty concentrating and the sugar cravings were obvious and quite intense. Everything inside me screamed out for food! Managing stress was a challenge, as I usually turned to candy or bingeing on other sugary or comfort foods to help me cope.

> **Serenity Prayer**
> God, Grant me the Serenity to accept the things I cannot change. The Courage to change the things I can; and the Wisdom to know the difference.

Since I had read about what to expect, I was able to recognize when the withdrawal symptoms started. By the 4th day, I had an intense headache and felt quite anxious. After I snapped at my spouse and kids, I felt ashamed of how I acted, which made me want to binge so I could numb those unwanted feelings. I decided I would eat just one cookie, and when I did, my withdrawal symptoms left! "I can do this," I told myself. "Just one cookie a day, and I can manage the symptoms!" Before I went to bed that night, I had eaten the entire plate of cookies and I felt so sick. Had I always felt this way after eating cookies and just had not noticed?

I reached out to my Accountability Partner, completed the exercise on slips and relapses*, and recommitted myself to my recovery and to getting through the withdrawals. As I realized I had never gone long enough without bingeing and eating sugar to get through the discomfort of the withdrawal, I recognized that there is no moderation for me. I cannot eat just one cookie. I really am addicted. I remembered something I had heard from a recovering food addict: "If you can't stop, don't let yourself get started." Now this made sense to me.

I will never forget those weeks of waiting for my withdrawal symptoms to subside. I was glad I had learned about withdrawal because I understood that the symptoms would eventually pass and I would get through it and feel better. Having this understanding gave me the hope and courage to tough it out just one day at a time until I could see the light at the end of the tunnel.

A few months later, I saw my physician who asked me how I was feeling. I told her I felt great, better than I ever had. My moods were more stable, I had energy, I didn't feel sick, and my aches and pains were gone. She said something to me that I will always remember: "Can you believe that the majority of people are walking around out there feeling the way you used to and thinking that it's normal?" It was a sobering thought.

*The exercise on slips and relapses can be found in the Defining Sobriety section of this workbook.

Tips for Managing Withdrawals

1. **Lean into the Pain**: While some tips to help you manage withdrawal will be provided, the truth is that you will just have to tough it out in order to get through it. You will need to "lean into the pain." Leaning in means that you acknowledge and face the discomfort of withdrawal; it means that you engage and deal with the real needs that you have. Knowing that you will live through it and that you will come out stronger than you were before helps you to continue on in your efforts. Our natural tendency is to "move away" from discomfort rather than to "lean into" it. Moving away means that we give in to the desire for a "fix" when the brain's reward center is crying out to be "drugged." However, if you will lean into the pain, acknowledging it and facing it head-on, you will allow your body and mind to detoxify. This will lead you to finally rid yourself of the withdrawal symptoms and the overwhelming desire to use food as a means of avoidance or escape.

    Richard Paul Evans in his book <u>The Walk</u> wrote:
    "The thing is, the only real sign of life is growth, and growth requires pain. So, to choose life is to accept pain. Some people go to such lengths to avoid pain that they give up on life. They bury their hearts, or they drug or drink (or eat) themselves numb until they don't feel anything anymore. The irony is in the end, their escape becomes more painful than what they are avoiding."

    In other words, the pain (discomfort) is not the problem. Running from the pain is the problem.

Every addict must pass through the withdrawal phase in order to recover.

2. **Keep Busy:** You will need some healthy ways to occupy yourself as you go through the withdrawal process. Keeping your hands busy can help you to not eat. Knit, color, build something, draw, golf, go a movie with a friend. All these activities and more can help you to get through the most difficult first week.

3. **An Accountability Partner:** You have previously heard us say: "Reach out or act out." What that really means is that by reaching out, you can find support to help you get through this. Otherwise, the stronger tendency is to "act out" or return back to our usual addict pattern with food and avoidance. This concept is particularly applicable to the withdrawal phase! Consider asking someone to be your Accountability Partner. You can ask a friend or you might find someone at a Twelve Step meeting for food addicts where they call this person a sponsor. An Accountability Partner is someone who will support your efforts to stay in recovery, to keep your Bottom Lines*, and to get back on track after a slip or a relapse. Talk to this person about your food addiction and how they can help you. Don't expect them to just know. Show them your book and what you are working on. It's a good idea to set some ground rules and structure with your Accountability Partner.

Here are some ideas of how your Accountability Partner might help you:

- Set up regular times to talk. This may be a phone call or getting together in-person. You may find it helpful in the beginning of your recovery to have daily contact with each other. And then as you gain strength and stability, contact once or twice a week may be all that is needed to support your growth process. Show them this workbook and what you are working on. Ask them to help you stay focused.
- Ask your Accountability Partner to talk with you about your goals and how you are doing on your Bottom Lines*. It is common for food addicts to avoid certain topics because they have slipped or relapsed. Give them permission to confront you about your avoidance. Let them know it's ok for them to bring up the "tough subjects."
- Encourage your Accountability Partner to not minimize your slips or relapses, even when you talk about them in a humorous way. There is nothing funny about food addiction but sometimes you may use humor to disguise discomfort or avoid the shame of your struggle.
- Ask them to check in with you regularly about how many days of sobriety you have.
- Ask them to help you set goals (Dailies) for regular self-care and encourage you to follow through with them.

*Bottom Lines are important part of recovery. You will set Bottom Lines in the Defining Your Sobriety Section.

4. **Attend a meeting:** If you haven't already, now is a good time to attend a Twelve-Step Meeting. You can search online for "Food Addiction" or "Celebrate Recovery" meetings that are available in

your area. Most communities will have a Twelve-Step Meeting of some kind every day of the week. If you need a meeting, just go. Don't worry if it is for alcoholism or drug addiction. If there isn't a food addiction meeting available on a day or at a time when you need one, just go and insert the words "food", "binge," and "eating" into the testimonials you hear. You may find this to be a very valuable support to your recovery work.

5. **Drink lots of water:** Your body likes water. Much of the time when we feel fatigued we are actually a bit dehydrated and just need water. Withdrawal can be serious business. Stay well hydrated.

6. **Move:** Get out and walk. Enjoy the fresh air. Walking can get the endorphins going; this can help you endure through the withdrawal process. Put on your headphones and listen to some uplifting music, podcasts, or a book as you walk. It's a win-win, and you can use this as one of your Dailies (Cor-condition: Movement).

7. **Get Enough Sleep**: Going through withdrawal is hard work and it can be exhausting for the body. Let's look at the importance of sleep and rest. Did you know that:

    - "We sleep as much as one-quarter less than our ancestors did, with average total sleep time decreasing from 9 hours in 1900 to less than 7 hours over the past 10 years.
    - In 2001, researchers found that sleeping less than 6 hours per night and remaining awake past midnight increased the likelihood of obesity.
    - In 2002, a study of 1.1 million people found that increasing body mass index (BMI) occurred when habitual sleep amounts fell below 7 to 8 hours." [18]

Some people seem to think it is some kind of badge of honor to not sleep! You might even hear others brag about how much they can do with very little sleep. Consider the real impact of not getting enough sleep. When we don't get enough sleep, we are impatient and irritable. We are more likely to make judgement errors. When we are fatigued, we naturally reach for carbs or for caffeine for energy or a "boost." Sleep is a good idea.

If you struggle with insomnia, here are some tips for better sleep:

Tips for Better Sleep
- Have a bedtime routine – include something relaxing, like light reading, to help you wind down.

---

[18] Georgini, N., (2011). Sleep Deprivation and Obesity…a relationship?, http://www.cursoer.com/en/sleep-deprivation-and-obesity-a-relationship

- Practice sleep meditation at bedtime. Mindfulness meditation exercises designed to promote sleep can be found online and are often helpful. This can also count for one of your Dailies! (Cor-condition: Mindfulness)
- Go to bed and wake up at the same time each day. Stay consistent on weekends too. The body loves consistency.
- Unplug in the evening*. The light from your electronics confuses your circadian rhythms, which affects your sleep cycle. It can also affect your cortisol (stress hormone) levels, causing insomnia and chronic inflammation which is linked to weight gain.
- No caffeine after 2:00 PM.
- No alcohol within six hours of bedtime.
- No sugar in the evening.
- Go to bed before midnight. The hours between 10:00 PM and 2:00 AM are the most beneficial and restorative.
- Sleep in a dark room. Keep the temperature cool and the room clean.
- Exercise regularly, but don't work out within three hours of bedtime.
- Remove work materials, TV, and computers from the bedroom.
- Use the bedroom for sleep and sex only. It confuses your mind and your body when you use your bed for eating, working, studying, TV, computer time, etc. It makes it harder to relax when you get into bed.
- Practice slow, deep breathing and focus on your breath.
- Memorize some poetry and recite it in your mind when you are having difficulty sleeping.
- Sleep Apnea testing could be appropriate at this time.

* If you must work on electronics in the evening, consider downloading software or purchasing special glasses that reduce the prominence of white–blue light during evening work.

A Word about Sleep Apnea: Sleep apnea is a potentially serious sleep disorder in which breathing repeatedly stops and starts again. Snoring may be a symptom of sleep apnea but is not always present. Sleep apnea is common in people with obesity. Most experts say as little as a 10% decrease in weight can lead to significant clinical improvement in the severity of sleep apnea. Successful treatment of sleep apnea – usually with continuous positive airway pressure (CPAP) – may reduce sleepiness, which then helps patients to more effectively lose weight[19]. Severe sleep apnea can be life-threatening. Undiagnosed or untreated sleep apnea can lead to serious complications, such as heart attack, glaucoma, diabetes, cancer, and cognitive and behavioral disorders.

If you live alone and struggle with obesity, you may not be aware that you stop breathing at night. Please see your health care provider about testing and treatment for sleep apnea.

---

[19] National Sleep Foundation, Obesity and Sleep. https://sleepfoundation.org/sleep-topics/obesity-and-sleep/page/0/2

TOOL: Surf the Urge

Urge surfing is a mindfulness-based relapse prevention tool coined by the late Dr. Alan Marlatt, a leading clinical psychologist in the field of addictive behaviors. The analogy is given that urges, or cravings, are like ocean waves. They swell up, get stronger, and then they begin to subside. This powerful tool will help you "surf the urge" to eat and better manage your cravings, just like a surfer rides the waves of the ocean rather than let the waves overtake them. It can also be used as one of your Dailies (Cor-condition: Mindfulness).

It is recommended that you search online for "Surf the Urge" or "Urge Surfing" and find a downloadable audio meditation to play whenever you have cravings. Listen to it frequently so that it becomes second nature to you.

How to Surf the Urge

1. Observe – What are you craving, feeling, or thinking?
2. Recognize, pay attention to and accept what is happening inside of you.
3. Breathe. Allow your body and mind to pause and plan your next steps.
4. Take time and allow your thoughts to expand so that you better understand and recognize what is going on with you. Look for helpful actions that will help you maintain your recovery.

Trust that the urge will pass.

JOURNAL ENTRY

Use this section to write down some of the thoughts and feelings you experience as you go through withdrawal. What will you do to manage your withdrawal symptoms?

_____

_____

_____

_____

_____

_____

Defining Your Sobriety

Sobriety in other addictions is easy to define: *"No matter what, I will not drink." "No matter what, I will not look at pornography."* The challenge with food addiction is that you still have to eat. You cannot say *"No matter what I will not eat."* The analogy of a tiger in the cage is a good one for food addiction: If you were a drug addict, you could put your drug in a cage, lock it up, and – although difficult – walk away. With food addiction, you have to take that tiger out of the cage at least three times a day and take it for a walk.

For food addicts, defining sobriety is a bit more difficult. It may vary from addict to addict in terms of what they can eat and still maintain sobriety. For example, some addicts will have a *"No matter what, I will not eat sugar"* statement that defines their sobriety. But while one food addict may find that they cannot eat any type of sugar or sugar substitute without it triggering a binge, another food addict may find they can eat honey or natural sugar substitutes like stevia or monk fruit without issue. Some food addicts may not be able to eat fast food at all, while other food addicts find that there are some fast food establishments that serve healthy options and are more easily managed.

The most successful recovering addicts are those who, in the very beginning of their recovery process, work on defining their sobriety. In other words, they ask themselves, "What will my sober life look life?" They do this by establishing Bottom Lines. A Bottom Line is what defines sobriety for you; it becomes your *"No matter what, I will/will not _____."* This section will help you
1) draw lines around your behaviors with food and
2) help you establish boundaries which define your sobriety and identify what you will and won't do.

Now that you have used the previous section to identify your food, location, and emotion triggers, you are ready to define your sobriety. Using your triggers as a guide, you can define what sobriety will look like for you. To get you started, most food addicts define their sobriety with their first Bottom Line as *"No matter what, I will not binge."*

Defining a Binge

Since most food addicts will set one of their bottom lines as: *"No matter what I will not binge,"* it is important to define what constitutes a binge. A binge is defined as the consumption of unusually large amounts of food in a relatively short period of time. Often this is at a time when you really are not hungry. Typically it is done alone, when no one can see or will know. It is not the same as overeating at dinner. It feels out of control. Once you get started, it feels impossible to stop. It is as if you get "in the zone" and are not even aware of what you are doing. Usually when you are finished you have some physical discomfort because you ate too much. There is also commonly a strong feeling of guilt and self-loathing. Your Shame Voice tells you that you are a failure or that you don't have enough willpower to stop. This is accompanied by feelings of disgust, depression, or mood swings.

A variation of binge-eating is consistently overeating throughout the day. Sometimes called "grazing", your binge happens over an entire day wherein you eat 7, 8, 9, or 10 times consuming many more calories than your body needs for fuel in the process.

Episodic binge-eating or grazing, at the end of the day you feel like you "totally lost control" over your eating.

Gateway Drugs

In addition to establishing a Bottom Line of not bingeing, defining your sobriety may take a trial and error approach as you continue to identify your triggers and establish healthier tools to help you. This helps you to further define what sobriety means for you. For example, be mindful of "gateway drugs." A gateway drug is a substance that may encourage the use of other drugs. For example, research shows that those who use marijuana are three times more likely to progress to heroin[i]. Many sex addiction specialists consider excessive use of video games to be a "gateway drug" to pornography use. The same can be said of certain foods. One recovering food addict noticed that whenever she added gluten back into her diet, it was only a matter of a week or two before she relapsed on sugar and was binge-eating. Another food addict found that eating chips and salsa triggered his craving for drinking sugary sodas. Trial and error is a powerful way to determine the "gateway drugs" that lead you to unhealthy eating or to another episode of binge eating.

Addiction Transfer

As you work to define sobriety, it will be important to watch out for addiction transfer. Addiction transfer simply means replacing one addiction for another. Since your addiction is not really about food, but about dopamine, you must be careful with other dopamine-producing activities. As many food addicts work to eliminate binge eating, they find that they are reaching frequently for their phones to play a game or to check social media[20], all of which produce dopamine. Other activities that can produce dopamine are pornography use, Internet surfing, gambling, and online shopping.

Additionally, if you have had a bariatric surgery, it is important that you understand how your body now metabolizes alcohol[21]. After surgery, the stomach enzymes that typically break down alcohol and release it into the blood stream are less able to do so. As a result, the effects of alcohol are felt more quickly and more intensely. If you have not dealt with the underlying issues of your food addiction prior to surgery, you may be at risk for developing an addiction to alcohol or some other substance. Many weight-loss surgeons

---

[20] 5 Crazy Ways Social Media Is Changing Your Brain Right Now, *AsapSCIENCE*, https://www.youtube.com/watch?v=HffWFd_6bJ0

[21] Parikh, M., Johnson, J., Ballem, N, (2016). ASMBS position statement on alcohol use before and after bariatric surgery, *Surgery for Obesity and Related Diseases*, 12, 225–230.

suggest that a patient abstain from alcohol for at least a year or longer following surgery and others encourage patients to stop using alcohol permanently.

Recognizing the difference between a slip and a relapse

As you establish your Bottom Lines and become more clear and specific regarding your definition of sobriety, it will be important to understand the difference between a slip and a relapse.
A slip has the <u>potential</u> to derail your sobriety and lead you off the path you have established. It means you crossed a line you have set for your lifestyle in sobriety. It is a "near miss."

A relapse is when you <u>lose</u> your sobriety. It is when you cross the line and stay there for a longer period of time. It is a fall; it is as though you have given in and let the addict return to old patterns of behavior with food.

For example, perhaps your sobriety states, *"No matter what, I will not binge,"* and you have an evening out with friends in which you overeat but you don't go fully into a binge. Overeating would be a slip. Because overeating can trigger a binge, it has the potential to derail your sobriety. Bingeing is a relapse – you have lost your sobriety, at least temporarily. If you were triggered by overeating at dinner, and on the way home you turned into the drive-thru, ordered all your favorite foods, and then went home and binged on them, you are in relapse.

Handling Slips and Relapses

Whenever you experience a slip or a relapse, it is an opportunity for you to learn something more about yourself that can strengthen your recovery moving forward. Take this opportunity to process your slip or relapse. That means you need to reach out and talk about your experience with someone or journal about it using the example below.

Exercise: Process your slip or relapse

After reading the sample, consider the following questions designed to help you process a slip or relapse. Write them down and share them with a friend, Accountability Partner, or with your therapist. Use these questions to strengthen your recovery anytime you have a slip or relapse.

SAMPLE:

What was happening before the slip?

I had been hoping that this guy in the office next to me would ask me out. He had been a bit flirty but nothing had happened yet. When my friends invited me to dinner, I was eager to go in an effort to get my mind off of this guy not asking me out.

What was I feeling?

I was excited about going to dinner with my friends; it had been a while since we had gotten together. I was also apprehensive. Restaurants can be difficult for me and I was already starting to obsess about what I would order. At dinner, the conversation turned to relationships and my friends asked if I was seeing anyone. All my friends are in a relationship except me. I felt left out of the conversation. I also felt rejection and anger – why hadn't that guy asked me out?

What thoughts accompanied these feelings?

My thoughts went to where they always go. "If I were thinner, he would want to go out with me," after which I felt angry that people are so judgmental and won't give people of size a chance. "I would make a good partner!" I declined dessert, but it was just for show. I was upset and already planning in my head to pick up a pizza and ice cream on my way home.

Identify the trigger (location, food or emotion):

The restaurant was a trigger for me. I have eaten there in the past and I always ate too much. The food on the menu and on the plates of the other patrons was a trigger – especially the mashed potatoes. Although this triggered me, I ordered steamed vegetables instead of the potatoes. At this point I was still doing well and feeling good about my progress in recovery. I thought about sharing some of the particulars regarding my addiction and my recovery efforts with my friends. However, it was the familiar emotions of rejection and anger, followed by the negative self-talk (thoughts) that ran through my head and led to my acting out. Those feelings triggered my relapse and took me down.

Is this a pattern for me when I have these thoughts and feelings? Do I typically reach for food at these times?

Yes, definitely! I can see it more clearly now. When I feel rejection and anger, I reach for food to make me feel better.

What will I do differently the next time I have a similar situation with these accompanying thoughts and feelings?

In the next few day I will let my closest friends know about my addiction and my recovery efforts so they can support me. I will risk being vulnerable with them and telling them my experience with this guy being flirty and not asking me out and how I felt when this happens. When I have emotional pain or negative self-talk come up in a social setting like this one, I will text my Accountability Partner that I need to talk after dinner. That will give me the support I need to not follow my old pattern and stop at the drive-thru for food on the way home.

What progress do I notice?

On my way to the drive-thru I thought "What am I doing? Do I really want to derail my sobriety?" Even though I did it anyway, I think the fact that I thought about it represents a slowing of the addictive process in my brain. Before, I would automatically go to the drive-thru with no conscious thought about what I was doing.

Use the following template of questions to process your last slip.

What was happening before the slip?

_____

_____

_____

_____

What was I feeling?

_____

_____

What thoughts accompanied these feelings?

_____

_____

_____

_____

Identify the trigger (location, food or emotion):

_____

_____

Is this a pattern for me when I have these thoughts and feelings? Do I typically reach for food at these times?

_____

_____

What will I do differently the next time I have a similar situation with these accompanying thoughts and feelings?

_____

_____

_____

_____

What progress do I notice?

_____

_____

_____

_____

Tip: Counting Days – Many food addicts will count their days of sobriety from their last binge, last sugar-fest, last whatever-it-is that defines their sobriety. There is something about not wanting to start over again that has helped many addicts to make it through another day. Look back and identify the date of your last binge – even if it is an estimated date – and mark this on your calendar. Let that represent the beginning of your sobriety and count the days as a way to encourage and support your efforts in recovery.

Bottom Lines

As mentioned, establishing Bottom Lines is key to defining your sobriety. Creating Bottom Lines helps you commit to specific behaviors in recovery. Part of the struggle with addiction is the tendency to rationalize or excuse our behavior; we explain it away and that allows us to "act out" in our addiction.

When you continue to follow your Bottom Line, it helps you to see the progress you have made. Bottom Lines support your efforts to be accountable to your recovery.

Recovery is a journey of growth and progress. As such, your Bottom Lines will change as you become more consistent in following them. Today, at the beginning of your recovery, they will be about specific behaviors such as the ones listed below. Later in your recovery, your Bottom Lines may address behaviors that, although they affect your recovery, may be harder to measure, such as: dealing with negative thoughts; how you cope with stress; not being evasive; being able to say "no;" or dealing with feelings of low self-worth.

A Bottom Line is different than a goal. A goal is something that you set to help you to improve or enhance your life and recovery. Your Dailies that come from the Cor-conditions are goals. A Bottom Line, on the other hand, defines your sobriety. It is a line that says, "I will not cross this line no matter what."

Here are some examples that show the difference between a goal and a Bottom Line:

Goal: *I will honor my hunger today and stop eating when I am no longer hungry.* (Cor-condition: Mindfulness).
Bottom Line: *No matter what, I will not binge.*

Goal: *I will work on my recovery reading for 20 minutes today.* (Cor-condition: Purposeful Activity)
Bottom Line: *No matter what, I will read or listen to something for my recovery every day.*

Goal: *Today I will cut up vegetables to keep in my fridge for this week.* (Cor-condition: Healthy Relationship with Food)
Bottom Line: *No matter what, I will plan my meals at least a day ahead.*

Goal: *I will schedule a time to meet with a friend one day this week.* (Cor-condition: Connection)
Bottom Line: *No matter what, if I have a slip, I will reach out and tell someone. I won't stay in hiding.*

Goal: *I will work on a craft project this evening instead of eating after dinner.* (Cor-condition: Play)
Bottom Line: *No matter what, I will not eat after 7:00 PM.*

Goal: *I will go to my water aerobics class today.* (Cor-condition: Movement)
Bottom Line: *No matter what, I will have a minimum of 150 minutes of movement each week.*

Can you see how Bottom Lines define sobriety?

Never Say Never
As you consider your Bottom Lines, you will want to be careful about the word "never." Just as an alcoholic cannot say *"I will never drink again,"* a food addict cannot say, *"I will never binge again."* The Twelve Step slogans of "One day at a time" and "Just for today" help addicts stay focused on what is happening

right now. While you may envision a time in your life when you will never binge again, change takes place in the present moment. *"For today, I will not binge."*

EXERCISE: My Bottom Lines

Start today by listing the specific behaviors that will define your sobriety – your Bottom Lines. Share this list with someone else. Just as in making New Year's resolutions, when you share your resolve with someone else, you are more likely to stay committed.

1. _____

_____

2. _____

_____

3. _____

_____

Define Your Sobriety

Now that you have your list, you can take your Bottom Lines and use them to define your sobriety. Let's take the Bottom Lines from the "Bottom Lines" section and use them to define one addict's sobriety. Perhaps it would sound like this:

I will know that I am sober when I do not binge, when I don't eat after 7:00 PM and when I consistently reach out for support if I slip.

EXERCISE: I will know I am sober when…

I will know that I am sober when:

_____

_____

_____

TOOL: BLAHST

BLAHST is an acronym that many support programs have used to help addicts recognize potential triggers. These are situations we come across every day that can lead to acting out in addiction.

Bored. Often when addicts start to look at their triggers, boredom is one that they identify. The next time you are bored pay attention to what you are feeling. More than likely in your quiet moments uncomfortable feelings come to the surface. Dealing with these feelings head on instead of stuffing them back down will give you more power over your addiction.

Loneliness. Everyone feels lonely at times but excessive loneliness can lead to isolation which is one of the enemies of recovery. The more you isolate, the more likely you are to binge. In recovery, you cannot afford to isolate! That is why it is so important to reach out to others. Connecting is a great strength in recovery.

Anger. Anger is a normal reaction to a perceived unfair situation. While it is normal to feel anger at times, it can dominate thoughts and emotions. It is difficult to think clearly when you are angry. Rather than "stuffing" your anger down with food, pick up a pen and journal, call a friend, read a book, or engage in a physical activity. Managing your anger in healthy ways promotes recovery.

Hungry. When you are hungry, your blood sugar drops, which can affect your emotional state of mind. Most people have difficulty concentrating when they are hungry and can be prone to erratic mood swings and impatience until their blood sugar is back to normal again. Don't skip meals. Eat on a regular schedule. Be consistent with this and it will help you sustain your recovery efforts.

Stressed. It has been said that stress is what helps us to know that we are alive but too much stress can cause you to reach for food to help you to cope with being alive! Recognizing that some stress is just a part of life can help you tie a rope and hang on. Learning to balance life, schedules, and relationships can help you deal with stress in healthy ways. Find other stress-reducing activities that don't involve food.

Tired. You need to think clearly in recovery and when you are tired you cannot process your thoughts well. When you are tired you are more likely to become impatient, resentful, and to reach out for carbs or caffeine to manage the fatigue. Sleep deprivation is also associated with weight gain. It may be tempting to stay up late, but late evenings are the most common time for emotional eating. When you are tired, rest.

JOURNAL ENTRY

Use this section to write down some of the thoughts and feelings about defining your sobriety. How will defining your sobriety help in recovery? Remember, structure and organization are good friends in recovery.

Developing a Healthy Relationship with Food

Like most food addicts you have probably had a love-hate relationship with food. This section will discuss some important concepts about having a healthy relationship with food and give you some concrete strategies to strengthen that relationship.

Understanding how your Relationship with Food has kept you from a having a Healthy Relationship with Yourself

Just like a jealous, controlling lover food has kept you from loving, being present with, being aware of, and taking good care of a very important relationship in your life – the one you have with yourself! Food has taken up your time and your energy; it has been the focus of your attention and it has been unyielding in its intent to keep you from paying attention to this other important and vital relationship. It has said to you: "I am all you need to focus on!"; "I am the best thing that has ever happened to you;" "There is nothing more important than me;" "I can give you everything you need;" "Without me you are nothing!" "You cannot figure things out on your own!" "You are not smart enough." The list of lies is extensive, and you have believed them.

As your jealous, controlling lover took over the first (second, third, etc.) priorities in your life, your own needs began to take a back seat and faded in importance to you. Your health, exercise, finances, dealing with your feelings, your social world, were all likely compromised because your jealous, controlling lover would not allow them to have a priority in your life. In time, all that was left was the abuser. As typically happens in this type of an abusive relationship, it all becomes about the jealous, controlling lover – keeping him or her calm and reassured. There is no room for you. The relationship becomes stifling, oppressive, and unyielding. It wears you down. You long to break free of it but you have been in it for so long and have believed the lies it has told you for so many years, you have little confidence that you possibly could, or would ever know how to break free.

If this sounds too harsh to you, consider for a moment the realities of the lifestyle that you have built for yourself in addiction. You live a busy, fast-paced and stressful life. You ignore or avoid things that are too unpleasant or difficult emotionally by using food to numb out or for comfort. You have believed that if you could just follow the diet program long enough you would have a better life... and that has not

> If you get the inside right, the outside will fall into place."
> -Eckhart Tolle

worked. You recognized that food is only a temporary soothing, comforting, distraction from the reality but you rationalized that it was "no big deal." Then you began to see some signs of a problem that you couldn't ignore – you've hit a weight that is the highest you've been. You can't seem to get rid of those extra pounds, no matter what you do. You have no time to cook or prepare a meal so you stop and pick it up on the way, or you skip it completely- only to overindulge later. Your last visit with the doctor was depressing. You learned that you are borderline diabetic, have hypertension, or some other health-related issue.

Can you see the picture? Are you really living the life you want for yourself? Maybe you are just sliding along on the surface of life never really digging into it. Finding joy and fulfilment seems so elusive. Maybe your relationships with others lack the depth of connection that you would find fulfilling. Maybe all those possessions you've acquired through your hard work and effort are not really all that rewarding or satisfying. Something is missing in your life and it's BIG. If you have feelings coming to the surface as you read this, you're not alone. Please resist the impulse to avoid what you are feeling right now. It can guide you to a new place of joy, confidence and freedom from food addiction.

EXERCISE: My Jealous, Controlling Lover

Take a minute to reflect on your unhealthy relationship with food. What has it kept you from doing or participating in? Who has it kept you from becoming? What needs have you been unable to meet because of it? Write down your thoughts and feelings that surface as you think about and ponder these questions.

Example:
"My unhealthy relationship with food has kept me from doing so many things. I long to travel, but I get so embarrassed about my weight and that I can't fit into an airplane seat that I talk myself out of going. I want friends, but I am afraid of their comments and judgments about my weight, spoken or unspoken. I know I will slow them down or not be able to do something they want to do and I will feel so guilty about that. My health is affected and I know I would feel better if I ended this toxic relationship with food. For years I have struggled with self-loathing because I have believed the lies this relationship has fed me about my own self-worth. I am tired of it, and I want out!"

_____

_____

_____

_____

EXERCISE: Good-bye Lover! Hello Me!

As your understanding has increased and you have been gaining some tools to deal with your food addiction, you are now ready to say good-bye to that collection of habits and patterns that have become so familiar in your day-to-day life. You can move forward with a healthy relationship with food ... and with yourself! Take a minute to reflect on what this new relationship might look and feel like. Then write it down so you can refer to it often.

Example:

"In my new relationship, I am free from the bondage of my jealous, controlling lover. I am in charge of my own life. I decide what I will eat and I consciously make food choices with the intent of fueling my body. I own my own feelings and allow others to do the same. I make healthy choices about how to use my time, and how best to take care of me and my needs! My health is improving and I can move more freely. I have a social life with friends who are supportive (not condescending) and with whom I can really connect. I had not realized how much my jealous, controlling lover was keeping me from living! Although I still have some work to do in dealing with my negative self-talk, staying conscious with my eating, and allowing my emotions to be expressed, I am on my way to a much better way of living, and it feels great. I am finding joy, confidence, and freedom from food addiction!"

_____

_____

_____

_____

With the unhealthy, obsessive relationship fading, you will find more mental space available to focus on developing a healthy relationship with food and eating. Below are some strategies to help you do this:

Strategy #1: Plan your meals and snacks ahead. This is a simple task that yields great results. Food addicts quickly find that by planning their meals and snacks at least a day ahead frees them from the daily obsessiveness around food. *"I don't think all day about what I am going to eat next when I have already made that decision!"*

Tip: Set aside a few minutes each day or week to plan what you will eat. Purchase needed items ahead of time and keep healthy foods available to minimize trips to the store. Remember the value of structure and organization; life gets simpler and easier when you have a plan and follow it.

Strategy #2: Shop for groceries online. Food addicts are triggered in the grocery store by all the aisles of food and the many delicious options. If you must go into a grocery store, shop the perimeter of the store (the produce, meat, and dairy sections) and try to stay out of the center aisles where most of the processed foods are kept. The less time you spend in a grocery store, the less likely you are to purchase unhealthy foods and have them in your home.

Tip: Download a grocery store online-shopping app. Keep it with you when you are preparing your food. When you see you are running low on an item, add it to your app. This helps you build a shopping list which is a tool to help you avoid impulsive purchases. It also saves time and you won't run out of the items you use most often. You can also save money as these apps keep a running shopping cart total. This will help you stay in your food budget. Also, remember that you never want to shop when you're hungry. Hunger leaves you more at risk for impulsive purchasing so if you have to go into a store, be sure you have already eaten.

Strategy #3: Make Your Environment Work for You. If you were an alcoholic, you wouldn't have alcohol in the home. If you gave up smoking, you wouldn't keep a pack of cigarettes in your purse or car. If you were addicted to pornography, you would put filters on your electronics to block access. Setting up your environment so that it works for you instead of against you is an important component in recovery for food addicts, most of whom are more likely to relapse in secret in their own homes rather than outside of it.

The best way to make your environment work for you is to remove the unhealthy foods from your home, car, and workplace. If necessary, ask a friend to come over and help you dispose of them. Remember sugary treats, French fries, processed foods, chips, cookies, cupcakes, pizza, soda, and other highly palatable foods put you at risk for relapse. In addition to triggering relapse, these processed foods also increase inflammation in the body which causes disease, physical pain and resistant weight. Use your list of trigger foods to help you with the process of deciding what to eliminate. Take an hour one day this week to pack them up and give them away or throw them out. But don't just get rid of the trigger foods, be sure to add some healthy snack alternatives into your environment that you like to eat.

"What!?" you might say. "My husband, the kids, and the dog are not going to be okay with this!" This statement is probably true and you may need to have a frank discussion with them ahead of time. The good news is that I have seen whole families become healthier. They start spending more time together in recreational activities because one of the parents worked to establish healthier practices in the home environment. Stand your ground! This is your recovery and in reality, it is your life. Make your environment work for you rather than against you.

Strategy #4: Don't get hungry. The registered dieticians with whom I consulted have all stressed this one very important thing – if you skip meals and wait until you are really hungry to eat, you are more likely to overeat. So, when you think you might be hungry use the "Am I Hungry?" tool found in the "Recovering Your Brain: Mindfulness" section to help you identify when it is time to eat. It's vital to know if you are physically hungry for food to fuel your body or if it is an emotional hunger that has been triggered and you need to do something else that does not involve food.

Strategy #5: Aim for half of your diet to be produce. Increasing your intake of fruits and vegetables will automatically decrease the amount of unhealthy food you consume. An easy way to eat healthy is to ensure that when you look at your plate, half of the food on it was grown and hasn't been processed. Lean towards the veggies more than the fruit.

Tip: Once a week, put on a podcast or music you like and take an hour to cut up fresh vegetables. Store these in a large, airtight container in the refrigerator for stir fry. When preparing a meal, toss a couple of handfuls into a wok with a little olive oil and sea salt and you have a great side dish! You can use these in a soup or for a healthy omelet too. Don't forget to cut up some crunchy vegetables and get them into lunch-size baggies for snacks or lunch at work. A little preparation ahead of time will make it easier to say "no" to yourself when tempted to just pick up fast food on the way home.

Strategy #6: Change *Just One Thing* a Week. You know the familiar adage to "Just take one thing at a time"? That is the heart of this strategy – just start with one thing and incorporate that into your lifestyle. The 22-week step-by-step Just One Thing Guide and Tracker found in the Addendum of this workbook were designed with the help of registered dieticians and will help you change your relationship with food.

Strategy #7: Don't Diet. This is an important directive. When you diet you are still obsessively thinking about food and forcing yourself to follow some regimen. "What can I eat on my diet today?" "How many calories or carbs does this food have?" "Should I use this oil or that one?" Compulsion is compulsion is compulsion. Your brain can't tell the difference between compulsively thinking about food and compulsively thinking about your diet, so it registers both the same way – as an addiction. Varying studies have shown that 95% of diets and weight-loss programs fail. Why? Diets don't treat addiction. Addiction treatment treats addiction. Stop dieting.

Strategy #8: Track Your Progress. Often, participants tend to focus on what is NOT going well with their recovery. In the Addendum of this book, you will find a "My Relationship with Food" scale. Using this scale to track your daily progress will help you to stay focused, recognize success, and recognize areas for improvement. This extra focus can also help you to recover more quickly. Be sure to write down your daily number from the scale into your *My Food Addiction Recovery Journal*.

When your brain has calmed from the addiction, has experienced some healing, and you have been successful at implementing *Just One Thing*, then it might be the time to add in a medically sound weight-loss program. If you decide to work with a registered dietician, ask them if they use the Trans-Theoretical Model of Change. This model looks much like the addiction cycle. Interview them first to be sure that they understand eating as an addiction and share your materials with them as you embark on the journey of working together.

Getting your loved ones on board

I have often heard comments from spouses and partners of food addicts like:

"But it makes him happy when I bring home a treat for him or make his favorite cookies."
"But that's what we do for date night – we go to dinner and a movie; and, of course, you have to have popcorn at the movies."
"It's one of our favorite things to do; we get the kids down for bed, get a bowl of ice cream and watch TV together."
"But it's Valentine's Day – what am I supposed to give her if I can't give her a box of her favorite chocolates?"

"What do I do when he or she gets upset or irritable? Or when she feels depressed? Food has always worked to make her feel better."

I encourage you to have a conversation with your loved ones and share what you are learning about food as an addiction. Compare it with drug use. Watch what happens when I take the above statements and insert the word "**cocaine**" in place of the food or eating activity:

*"But it makes him happy when I bring home **cocaine** for him."*
*"But that's what we do for date night – **cocaine**. Of course you need to have **cocaine** at the movies."*
*"It's one of our favorite things to do; get the kids down for bed, use **cocaine** and watch TV together."*
*"But it's Valentine's Day – what am I supposed to give her if I can't give her **cocaine**?"*
*"What do I do when he or she gets upset or irritable? Or when she feels depressed? **Cocaine** has always worked to make her feel better."*

This is a serious and potentially life-threatening addiction. Help your loved one to see it that way.

Then have a fun conversation about transforming your relationship. Here is what other food addicts in recovery have done in their relationships that doesn't include food:

- Write a love note on a post-it and put it on the bathroom mirror or their pillow.
- Change date night to a walk in the park instead of a restaurant.
- Take a painting class together.
- Ride bikes.
- Get the kids down, put on a little soft music and have a conversation about the positive aspects of your day. Share your appreciation for each other by talking about the things in your relationship that bring you joy.
- Flowers are just as great as chocolates on Valentine's Day. They last longer and there is no guilt associated!
- Take a stroll together through the mall in your best disguises and see if anyone recognizes you.
- Find something that will make you laugh together.
- Ask for what you need: "Will you take a walk with me?" "Let's take a ride." "I need a nap."

JOURNAL ENTRY

Use this section to write down some of the thoughts and feelings you are experiencing as you reviewed this section on "Developing a Healthy Relationship with Food." Consider the Strategies and the *Just One Thing* tool found in the Appendix.
Ask yourself:
- Where will the obstacles be?
- How will I overcome them?
- What parts will be easy?
- What might I feel as I implement *Just One Thing* in my life?

- What will I do to help my loved ones to get on the same page with my and better understand and support my recovery efforts?

Additional Tips for a Successful Recovery

In addition to the exercises and suggestions that you have already been working on in this workbook, this section will provide you with additional recovery tips that have been beneficial to other food addicts in recovery. It is by no means a comprehensive list. Include other helpful suggestions you find along your path to recovery. Use your journal as a place to write about and explore how these tips and exercises benefit you. Return to this section again and again as you implement these different tips and principles into your recovery.

My Travel Plan

When we travel our schedules and routines are disrupted and the temptation to take a break from recovery is real. Recovery doesn't take a vacation (or a business trip for that matter). Does this mean you can't travel? Of course not! But travel is not an excuse for letting go of one's recovery. As your brain is busy building new, healthy neural pathways it continues to need the structure that your *My Food Addiction Recovery Journal* and this workbook provide to you. Adapt your Dailies to your trip and activities. Use your journal every day and keep tracking your Dailies. Your brain will thank you for it! Here are some ideas for a successful recovery-trip.

1. **Plan for fun -** Many food addicts have shared that they have often planned their vacations around places they want to eat. When you take your next vacation change your focus from food to visiting interesting places that you want to see and doing some of the fun things that are available. No food tourism! Research "things to do" in the cities you will be visiting before you go. Find engaging activities available, like cycling, kayaking, hikes, movies, miniature golf, concerts, visiting local museums, riding a Segway, taking a river tour, or visiting a botanical garden! Take the focus off the food and put it on the FUN. (Cor-condition: Play)

   > Recovery doesn't take a vacation. Plan ahead!

2. **Prepare ahead for location triggers** – Restrooms are typically placed inside of gas station mini-stores which are full of unhealthy, triggering foods: chips, candy, cookies, hotdogs and soda, etc. Put on your imaginary blinders and head for the restroom and then get out of there quickly! Additionally, rest stops typically have vending machines. Stay away from even browsing. There is nothing in them you can eat so don't fire up the Preoccupation Stage of the Addiction Cycle by "just looking." Of course, you will want to be careful with the visit to "Aunt Sally" who believes food is love. She will insist that you eat her home-cooked meal or indulge in her plate of delicious chocolate chip cookies. Her intentions may be good, but don't let it derail your recovery. Rehearse conversations ahead of time in which you say "no" to Aunt Sally and commit to using your gentle, but firm responses. (Cor-condition: Healthy Relationship with Food)

3. **Making your hotel environment work for you** – A little advanced planning can safeguard your recovery when staying in a hotel.

- **Hotel Room:** Call ahead to request a mini-fridge in your room. Ask for a microwave if that's available too. If flying, head for a nearby grocery store as soon as possible after you arrive. Stock the refrigerator with the food you packed or purchased. Whole foods, nuts, veggies, fruit, string cheese, deli meat slices, whole grain bread, almond butter, and fruit-sweetened jam are just a few examples of the possibilities you can easily keep in a hotel room. Pack a couple of plastic knives and forks as well. Be sure to have plenty of water for your water bottle and stay well hydrated on your trip. (Cor-condition: Healthy Relationship with Food)

- **Movement Minutes**: Use the hotel fitness center for your movement minutes. Take your phone along and listen to some uplifting music or an interesting podcast while you are working out. No fitness center? Dancing or yoga with a You-Tube video on your tablet in your room can be a great alternative. Better yet, head out for a walk and see the sights! Be sure to track your minutes in your **My Transformation Journal**. (Cor-condition: Movement)

- **Eating healthy at the complimentary breakfast-buffet:** These buffets are laden with high sugar, high-fat pastries and other unhealthy foods, but they often include healthy choices. Think protein and a healthy carb for energy; oatmeal with peanut butter, sausage/egg with fruit, banana with peanut butter, yogurt with fruit, etc. (Cor-condition: Healthy Relationship with Food)

4. **Prepare ahead for travel times** – Don't count on being able to find healthy food while you are in transit. Bring a light, small cooler with a shoulder strap and pack healthy foods for the trip in the car, plane, or on the train. Pack raw veggies, nuts, fresh fruit, low-fat string cheese, hard-boiled eggs, sandwiches on whole-grain bread, yogurt, etc. (Cor-condition: Healthy Relationship with Food)

5. **Eating in Restaurants** – Be sure to choose meal options where at least half of your plate is non-starchy produce. Portion sizes in restaurants are often enough for 2-3 meals, so ask your server for a box at the beginning of your meal. This allows you to manage the portion size before you even start to eat. Once you return to your hotel, keep your leftovers in the fridge for a meal the next day. You could also share a meal with a travel companion and not have to deal with leftovers. (Cor-condition: Healthy Relationship with Food)

Exercise: My Personal Travel Plan

Think about the triggers you will have on the trip and use the space below to make a plan:

Potential Trigger:

_____

I will handle this by:

_____

Potential Trigger:

I will handle this by:

Potential Trigger:

I will handle this by:

Potential Trigger:

I will handle this by:

Potential Trigger:

I will handle this by:

Safe and fun travels!

Track Your Movement Minutes

As you learned in the Recovering Your Brain section, you want to work up to a minimum of 150 minutes of physical activity or exercise each week. It's important and fun to track your movement minutes so that you can see how you are progressing with this important goal. Before beginning check out Dr. Mike Evan's video titled 23½ hours https://www.youtube.com/watch?v=aUaInS6HIGo about the amazing health benefits from just walking 150 minutes a week. Also remember to get your physician's okay before embarking on any new exercise plan.

Here are some suggestions for easy ways to track your progress:

- The best place to track your Movement Minutes is in your *My Food Addiction Recovery Journal*. Space is provided there for you to account for your minutes each day.

- A space is also included for you to track Movement Minutes on your *Just One Thing Tracker* in the Appendix of this workbook. This allows you to see your overall progress over 22 weeks.

- A wearable technology device that records your activity can be fun to use.

- Tracking apps are also available for your smartphone. Download several of them, try them out, and use the one you like best.

Recovery Reading

While you are the one who chooses your Dailies for the Cor-conditions each day, it is highly recommend that one of your Dailies always be to do some Recovery Reading for the Cor-condition: Purposeful Activity. Read for at least 10 minutes a day. The following are some suggestions for Recovery Reading Dailies:

- Read in this workbook and complete the exercises.
- Read or listen to articles, talks, books and podcasts about food addiction.
- Read or listen to motivational self-help books, talks and/or podcasts.
- Listen to motivational podcasts and talks on recovery and overcoming addiction.

Recovery Slogans

Recovery slogans are quick, catchy phrases that help to keep you focused on recovery and its accompanying principles. Here are some of my favorites:

> No more Mondays

"*One day at time*" reminds us that we only have to stay sober for today. Recovery becomes more manageable and far less overwhelming to face one day at a time, rather than to wrestle with the pressure of doing this for the rest of your life.

"*Abstinence (sobriety) is a journey and not a destination*" reminds us that we don't have to be perfect; we just have to keep going in the right direction.

We are reminded that doing what we used to do doesn't get us where we want to go with "*Old behaviors lead to old behaviors.*"

When we slip or relapse, we tend to tell ourselves that we will just start over again on Monday and then eat all our favorite, unhealthy foods between now and Monday. "*No more Mondays*" helps us to know that the time to start over again is right now.

"*You can't change what you can't see*" encourages us to look at the behaviors that are keeping us stuck in food addiction and make necessary changes.

For this fun exercise, go online and search for "recovery slogans" or "Twelve Step slogans" and make a list of some recovery slogans that will help you along the road to recovery. Write them down here on this list. You can also write them on post-it notes and place them on your mirror, in your car, or on the refrigerator door where you will see them often.

1. _____

2. _____

3. _____

4. _____

5. _____

6. _____

Staying on Track on Stressful Days

Wouldn't it be great if everything in life would just stop while you are in recovery so you can focus your efforts on just that… your recovery? But it doesn't. There will still be crises, stressors, work deadlines, and overwhelming experiences to deal with on any given day.

Maintaining your daily structure with the help of your *My Food Addiction Recovery Journal* will be a very helpful strategy. When life throws you a curve, adapt your Cor-cards for simpler Dailies. For example, adapt your Recovery Reading Daily from one page to a half of a page in your workbook. Instead of cutting up your vegetables, set a Daily to pick-up some pre-cut vegetables. If your schedule isn't allowing for a 30-minute walk that day, adapt your Daily to walk for 15 minutes at your lunch break and a 15-minute walk after work. It will be helpful to maintain your structure and plan while still allowing for some adjustments for more difficult and demanding days. Remember, this doesn't mean you "failed;" it means you are smart and courageous enough to maintain your focus on recovery while being adaptable to challenges that arise.

TIP: It's a good idea to have a few pre-written adapted "Stressful Day Cor-cards" so when you feel overwhelmed, instead of "throwing in the towel" you are prepared with a plan!

Self-care – How often do you put the needs of others ahead of your own? How often do you struggle to do the things that are necessary for your own well-being? Taking care of yourself is an important principle in recovery. It's a good example for your kids and family. It will lead you to reap some great rewards and strengthen your recovery.

Take the Cor-cards for example – each of the 9 Cor-conditions are a form of self-care:

- **Purposeful Activity** helps you grow as you learn new things about recovery.
- **Mindfulness** helps you stay in the present moment, rather than feeling anxious about the future or depressed about the past.
- **A Healthy Relationship with Food** nourishes your body including your brain.
- **Connection:** As you share and connect with others, you feel uplifted, encouraged, and loved.
- **Self-compassion** teaches you to view your mistakes as a means for growth, to talk to yourself with love and encouragement instead of trying to shame yourself into doing the right thing.
- **Movement** helps circulation, gets your heart rate going, strengthens muscles, decreases inflammation and provides healthy endorphins to help clear your mind and feel uplifted.
- **Play** rejuvenates you.
- **Music** can uplift you or it can help you to relax.
- **Service** gets you up and out of your own head. Helping someone else can be a good reminder that others also have problems and need help too. It gives perspective.

Can you see how the Cor-conditions are really categories for self-care and not just a list of things you have to get done each day? Our cultural belief tells us that our self-worth is determined by the things we accomplish or achieve. In other words, our value is linked to the number of things we can check off our To D0 list. Your Dailies are not a To Do list – they are a Self-Care list. The more you do things on this list, the more you take care of yourself and affirm your own value and worth.

My Holiday Plan

Holidays are full of fun events and being with family and friends! They are also full of traditional foods that we love and associate with good, happy memories. Holidays are a trigger time for food addicts. Over-eating and sugary foods are highly associated with holidays, birthdays and other celebrations.

Here are some suggestions to help you feel good about both a special event and your recovery:

- Don't arrive hungry. In the past you may have chosen not to eat before the event to "save room" for your favorite foods. We eat more when we let ourselves get too hungry so be sure to eat something ahead of time. **(Cor-condition: Healthy Relationship with Food)**

- Eat mindfully. We all love holiday foods, so enjoy them! Eat them slowly. Take time to savor the flavor. Think about how grateful you are for the food, the holiday, and those around you. (Cor-condition: Mindfulness)

- Stay hydrated. We get pretty busy during holiday seasons and forget to drink as much water as we need. Keep your water bottle with you. **(Cor-condition: Healthy Relationship with Food)**

   > Make a Memory Holiday

- Got a food-pusher ("drug dealer") in the family? Rehearse conversations in advance in which you turn down food. Remember, you don't owe anyone an explanation unless you desire to discuss your recovery with them.

- Change your focus from a "food-holiday" to a "memory-holiday"." Here are some examples from other recovering food addicts shared with their permission:

  - One decided to make non-food items for her neighbors for Christmas rather than giving the traditional plate of home-baked cookies and candy. She and her husband shared lasting memories of their interactions with their neighbors that year. (Cor-condition: Service)

  - A recovery group decided they would eat small portions of the foods they love for Thanksgiving Dinner and then go for a walk afterwards, rather than dropping on the couch uncomfortable from over-eating. When they returned to group, they shared how wonderful it was to have what they called their first "Compulsion-free Thanksgiving." They happily described how others joined them for the walk and the sweet, meaningful conversations they had! (Cor-condition: Movement)

  - A couple brainstormed new ways to show love on Valentine's Day without chocolates and had a special date where they walked in the park, held hands and talked about their plans for their healthy future. (Cor-condition: Connection)

- Most communities will hold special events near or on holidays such as a "Jingle Bell Run" or a "Turkey Trot." Some participants have set goals to participate in the 2-mile walk or 5k-run portion of these events and worked towards it for several months before the event. This helped them to stay focused on their Movement goals and they had a really fun time! (Cor-condition: Movement)

Good memories sustain us during difficult times. They comfort us when loved ones have passed on. Make holidays "memory-days" in your life! Stay present emotionally. Take time to talk with each person who attends. Say something encouraging in each conversation. Making memories to hold in your heart changes holidays from food-focused to memory-focused events.

Exercise: My Personal Holiday Plan

Think about the triggers you will have at the next holiday and use the space below to plan how you will manage them:

Potential Trigger:

_____

I will handle this by:

_____

_____

Potential Trigger:

_____

I will handle this by:

_____

_____

Potential Trigger:

_____

I will handle this by:

_____

_____

My Food Addiction Recovery Journal– The *My Food Addiction Recovery Journal* is available as a companion to this *My Food Addiction Recovery Plan*. This special journal gives you a place to reflect daily on your growth and consider next steps, track your progress, and keep you inspired in doing the things that matter most for recovery and transformation! Studies show that the process of writing slows our brain and is healthy for it so be sure to count this as one of your dailies! (Cor-condition: Mindfulness)

Purchase the *My Food Addiction Recovery Journal* at: **amazon.com/author/staceybthacker**

Recovery Playlist

You learned in the section on "Recovering Your Brain" that music has a positive effect on the addicted brain. My food addiction recovery groups have found it both useful and uplifting to create a personalized playlist of "recovery songs." Make your own Recovery Playlist by choosing songs that speak recovery to you or that encourage you. Talk to others about songs that lift them up and consider them for your playlist as well. Search on YouTube for "recovery songs." As you find new songs, add them to your playlist. Listen to them at key points of your day, such as while you are getting dressed in the morning, driving in the car, out walking, while you are preparing your food or if you find your mood dropping and feel triggered.

Be sure to write in a Daily for Music on your Cor-card in your *My Transformation Journal*!
(Cor-condition: Music)

What are some songs that you will include in your Recovery Playlist?

1. _____

2. _____

3. _____

4. _____

5. _____

6. _____

Create Your Own Personal Support System

A support system is crucial to success when you are in recovery. It gives you a place to talk about your struggle, share your victories, and ask for help. It gives you someone to whom you can be accountable for reporting your progress on your Bottom Lines, for maintaining the structure of your recovery (Dailies and Cor-cards), and your sobriety.

Exercise: Circle of Support

Consider the people who you already know that you might include in your Circle of Support. Are they empathic? Good listeners? Non-judgmental but still able to confront you when you slide off the path? Will they help you to become more honest with yourself about your struggle with food and eating? Will they encourage you to get back on track if you slip and you make a joke about it? Will they sabotage your recovery by inviting you to go for ice cream "just this once"?

It is unrealistic to think that any *one* person can be there for you *all* of the time. It's a good idea to have several (or more!) support people that you can reach out to when you need support.

Use this circle to brainstorm and then list some of the people that you think might be helpful in your Circle of Support. Consider the different settings of your life, such as family, work, social contacts, church, etc. It can be good to have someone in each setting when possible.

Note: I have noticed that although spouses want to be supportive, they may have difficulty in being objective because they are too close to the situation. It's not always a good idea to have a spouse or partner be the one to hold you accountable for your sobriety.

When you have decided who you would like to invite into your Circle of Support, meet with them individually or collectively and share information about your food addiction and your efforts in recovery. Be vulnerable and honest. Ask them if they have the time and would accept the invitation to be there for you in recovery. Let them know that it is okay if they can't make a commitment at this time. Also, tell them that you will ask several people. That way it isn't too much for any one person and they don't feel that they must drop everything to help you if you are struggling and they are not available.

Talk with them about what you will need. A daily check-in via text? A weekly conversation on the phone or in person? While you should be responsible for initiating the contact, would you like them to check in if they don't hear from you for a few days and to specifically ask if you are on track? Will they call you on any rationalizing, minimizing, or denying to help you see what you doing? This will go better if you can be clear about what you will need from them and elicit their commitment to join your Circle of Support.

What do you feel you will need from your Circle of Support?

_____

_____

_____

_____

Your Emotional Bank Account

Some activities fill us up. Some activities drain us. Although there will always be some things that you have to do that you may not enjoy, if your day, work, or life is filled with things (or people) that drain you, it will lead to burnout, depression, and resentment. The following exercise is designed to help you identify and make necessary changes to take care of yourself emotionally.

Exercise: The Check Register for Emotional Dollars

Take out an old paper check register (that comes with your checks), a three-column ledger sheet or note pad:
- Write down everything you do for seven days.
- Decide if each one is a debit OR a credit.
- Give it a dollar value and post that in the register.
- After seven days, run the numbers; you'll see if you are in the red (debit) or in the black (credit).
- The end result is you will have a list of what <u>fills you up</u> and what <u>drains you</u>.

Think of what you know about financial management: credits need to exceed deficits or you will find yourself in the red-in debt or worse yet bankrupt. That is a very difficult place to be financially. It is a very challenging place to be emotionally as well. We tend to make bad decisions from a place of emotional deficit.

This is a skill you can learn. Just like you use your check register to know where you are financially, you can do the same with your Emotional Bank Account. Take the challenge! The results will be insightful in helping you recognize when you are not doing enough self-care. You will see where there are places to cut back or increase to help you find the necessary balance.

Twelve-Step Meetings – These meetings were developed by the founders of Alcoholics Anonymous (A.A.) to provide support for those overcoming alcoholism. The program gained success and other addiction-focused support groups designed themselves after the A.A. model. Twelve-Step Groups for food addiction include but are not limited to: Food Addicts Anonymous, Overeaters Anonymous, Food Addicts in Recovery Anonymous, and Compulsive Eaters Anonymous-H.O.W. and more. These free and valuable groups provide a setting for open sharing of the struggle and the success of overcoming food addiction. You may also find faith-based groups – such as Celebrate Recovery, LDS Addiction Recovery Program or other religion-focused groups – where similar support help is available at no cost. If you have had weight-loss surgery, many of the hospitals or surgical practices have support groups to help their patients stay on a compliant path through their post-surgery journey of lifestyle change.

Choosing an Accountability Partner or Sponsor
In a Twelve-Step group, you are encouraged to choose someone to be your Sponsor. A sponsor is an accountability partner, someone with whom you check in regularly to report your progress. Different than a friend in your Circle of Support, this person has some experience with recovery and has had success in overcoming food addiction. They should be familiar with the Twelve Steps and be ready and willing to lead you through them.

Put together a group
With 70 percent of Americans overweight, we can assume that a great many of them are struggling with food addiction. Approach some friends and see if they would be interested in meeting to go through the My Food Addiction Recovery Plan Workbook and it's companion *My Food Addiction Recovery Journal*. There is strength in numbers and it could be fun!

Therapy

Many people find that when they give up addictive behaviors, long-buried emotions begin to surface. Try not to let this frighten or trigger you into giving up. See it as a great opportunity for growth and fine a therapist in your community. Look for someone who is interested in working with people who struggle with their relationship with food or eating, recognize it as an addiction, and who are willing to help you with this workbook.

Remember, regardless which of these suggestions you choose for your Personal Support System, be sure to include these planned interactions as a Daily on your Cor-cards for Connection!

Stay Away from the Edge

A story is told of a company that wanted to hire a new truck driver. The route this driver would have to take involved driving over a mountain on winding roads.

The first interviewee came in and the question was asked, "How close to the edge can you drive?" Confidently, he responded, "I can drive within one foot of the edge!?"

The second interviewee was asked the same question. "How close to the edge can you drive?" He responded, "I have driven for many years and have lots of experience driving close to the edge. I can drive closer to the edge than anyone you have seen."

> *The virtue of all achievement is victory over oneself. Those who know this victory can never know defeat."*
> *-Archibald J. Cronin*

The third interviewee was asked, "How close to the edge can you drive?" He responded, "Sir, I will treat your truck as if it were my own. I will not get anywhere near that edge!" HE was successful at obtaining the job.

With addictions, there is a tendency to want to live on the edge of recovery. Over the next several months, you will attempt to convince yourself many times that you do not have an addiction; that you can eat just one lunch-size bag of chips; that other people can eat sugar in moderation, so you should also be able to as well. The voice that will be loudest in your head will be, "I am not an addict!" <u>Rationalization is the biggest "edge" in those first weeks of recovery.</u>

Stay away from the edge!

Life has many guidelines, rules, and principles that are designed to keep us safe, like not driving close to the edge. Recovery is about principles. Although we can choose which principles we want to follow, we cannot choose the consequences. If you follow the principles of recovery that you have learned in this workbook you will have a greater probability of achieving success through your efforts.

JOURNAL ENTRY

Use this section to write down some of the thoughts and feelings you have had while studying the tips and principles taught in this section. What do you think will be different in your life as you implement them?

Next Steps

The *My Food Addiction Recovery Plan* is a great self-help workbook. Add in therapy to help you uncover the blocks that keep you stuck in your addiction and you have a great resource for success. If you find this is not sufficient for you or you would just like some additional resources check out these additional workbooks:

JOURNAL ENTRY

Use this section to write down some of your thoughts and feelings about finishing this workbook. Answer the following questions:
What will I do next to continue my recovery?
Where can I find needed resources?

_____

_____

_____

_____

_____

_____

_____

_____

_____

_____

ADDENDUM

Healthy Relationship with Food Tune-in Scale

Tune into you each day and rate where you are with your relationship with food on a scale from 1-5. Write it in your My Transformation Journal. Don't focus on perfection – just progress!

1. I was really struggling with my relationship with food today. I did a lot of emotional eating. I didn't reach out for support. I wasn't very aware of how much, what, or when I was eating*. I may or may not have skipped meals. I will write out my food plan for tomorrow right now. Tomorrow will be better! I am not giving up.

2. I had a difficult time with my relationship with food today but I did feel more aware ☺! I binged* and ate late at night, but I was aware that I was doing it. I didn't reach out for support. I skipped a meal and/or didn't plan my food in advance. I will write out my food plan for tomorrow right now. I got this one!

3. My relationship with food improved today. I ate mindfully some of the time. I overate at least once but was aware that I was doing it and I didn't go into a binge*. I added some healthy foods to my meals and snacks. I may or may not have reached out for support. I ate breakfast. I am writing out my food plan for tomorrow right now. I am moving forward ☺!

4. I had a good relationship with food today☺! I ate mindfully much of the time. I didn't binge*. I didn't eat late at night and I ate healthy foods about 75% of the time. If I was struggling this week, I reached out. Some of the time, I honored my hunger by eating something when I was hungry and stopping when I feel satisfied. I am doing it!

5. My relationship with food was great today ☺! Most of the time I honored my hunger by eating something when I was hungry and stopping when I felt satisfied. I ate mindfully more often than not. I ate foods to nourish my body and give me energy 90-100% of the time. I didn't eat after 7:30 PM. If I was struggling today, I reached out for support. I am consistently planning my meals ahead and I'm feeling better every day!

*Overeating and a binge is not the same thing. A binge is defined as the consumption of unusually large amounts of food in a relatively short period of time. See Defining Your Sobriety.

Just ONE Thing

Creating a Healthy Relationship with Food

THIS IS NOT A DIET PLAN. It is important that you implement the following changes consistently but not with the rigor of a calorie or carb-counting diet. Your brain cannot tell the difference between compulsive dieting and compulsive eating. For your brain to heal from compulsivity (addiction) you must give up compulsions. Making just one change a week can help you create a healthier relationship with food, give you time to adjust to each change and heal your brain from addictive behaviors.

As you move into each week, keep the change from the week before. For example, if in Week 1 you increase your daily water intake, then in Week 2 you would add Walk 10 minutes a day AND keep your increased water intake and so on through the 20 weeks.

Don't change what you are already eating until you get to a week that gives you a nutritional change. Keep doing the healthy things you are already doing.

Remember to consult with your physician or health care provider before beginning any new exercise or nutritional plan.

Week 1: Enjoy at least 9 cups of water a day if you are female, 13 if you are a male.
The Institute of Medicine determined that an adequate intake for men is roughly 13 cups of total beverage a day and about 9 cups for women. [i]
(COR-Condition Daily: Healthy Relationship with Food)

Week 2: Walk for 10 minutes 3x this week
Movement enhances emotional wellbeing and overall health[ii]. Walking is a great place to start. If 10 minutes is too much, split it up and walk twice for 5 minutes each time. If walking is too difficult, get an office chair with wheels, sit in it and start by rolling it on your kitchen floor!
(COR-Condition Daily: Movement)

Week 3: Eat at least 2 vegetables a day
Raw, steamed, grilled or baked, we feel good about eating vegetables! Make sure these are non-starchy vegetables and start thinking dark green and leafy!
(COR-Condition Daily: Healthy Relationship with Food)

Week 4: Use the "Am I Hungry?"
With one hand on your heart and the other hand on your gut, ask yourself "Am I Hungry?" Do you feel it in your stomach or in your chest? If it's in your chest, it's not food you need, it's emotional hunger. Ask yourself "What do I really need right now?" Call a friend, take a walk, take a break. Do this at least once a day when you are thinking about eating something.
(COR-Condition Daily: Mindfulness)

Week 5: Add in 2 fruits a day
Hopefully you will already eat fruit, but if not let's add it in to your daily nutritional plan. When you start limiting process sugar, you will notice your taste buds returning to normal. Fruit tastes much sweeter now!
(COR-Condition Daily: Healthy Relationship with Food)

Week 6: Are you eating 3 servings of whole grains a day?
The Whole Grains Council recommends we eat 3 servings of whole grains a day. What is a serving? Here are a few examples:
- 1/2 cup cooked brown rice or other cooked grain
- 1/2 cup cooked 100% whole-grain pasta
- 1 slice whole grain bread
- 1/2 cup cooked hot cereal, such as oatmeal[iii]

(COR-Condition Daily: Healthy Relationship with Food)

Week 7: Honor your Hunger
You may have heard it said that you have to eat to lose weight. It's true. When we get too hungry, we tend to overeat. This week increase your awareness of when your body needs fuel. Tune into your hunger and honor it. If you feel hungry or light headed, eat! But stop when you are no longer hungry! This simple tool is the most important one for weight loss.
(COR-Condition: Mindfulness)

Week 8: Be sure you are eating adequate protein each day.
Check out the My Plate website at: http://www.choosemyplate.gov/food-groups/protein-foods.html to see how much and what kind of protein you should be eating each day for your gender, age and activity level. Remember, when it comes to meat think lean!
(COR-Condition Daily: Healthy Relationship with Food)

Week 9: Eat 5x a day
Small, frequent meals help keep your blood sugars level and avoid the highs and lows of mood. Not allowing yourself to get too hungry will help you to not overeat. Remember: You have to eat to lose weight!
Exception: if you are post weight-loss surgery, you should continue or return to your surgeon's recommendations for amounts and frequency during this week.
(COR-Condition Daily: Healthy Relationship with Food)

Week 10: Add another 10 minutes to your walk and bump it up to 4x a times (Total 20 minute walk).
Woo hoo! You are on your way to health! Invite a friend, listen to uplifting music- make this part of your self care!
(COR-Condition Daily: Movement)

Week 11: Add in an orange or yellow vegetables every day!
Carrots, orange and yellow bell peppers, yellow or spaghetti squash are just a few of the delicious vegetables in the Orange/Yellow category.[iv] (COR-Condition Daily: Healthy Relationship with Food)

Week 12: Are you consuming the equivalent of 3 cups of dairy each day?
For healthy bone strength, you want to be sure you are getting calcium-rich and Vitamin D foods like milk, yogurt and cheese. Check out the My Plate website to see what foods would equal the 1- cup requirement http://www.choosemyplate.gov/food-groups/dairy-counts.html such as 2 slices of hard cheese (3 ozs) is equivalent to 1 cup of milk.
(COR-Condition Daily: Healthy Relationship with Food)[v]

Week 13: Tune-In to You at every meal.
You have been doing the Tune Ins at your group sessions. This week add them into your meal ritual before each meal by asking yourself "How am I feeling physically, emotionally and spiritually?
(COR-Condition Daily: Mindfulness)

Week 14: Cut up veggies once a week and add 1 more serving a day
Set aside a half hour and turn on some inspiring music! Cut up all your veggies for snacks, stir-fry, and other dishes and store them in plastic containers or baggies in the fridge. You are more likely to use them if they are prepared ahead! **Now you can say that "1/2 my diet is produce"!** Congratulations!
(COR-Condition Daily: Healthy Relationship with Food)

Week 15: Eat for Fuel
Processed foods like white flour and sugar products are high in addictive ingredients and drain your energy. Eat a healthy carbohydrate with a protein and you will notice a difference in your energy level. Try an apple with peanut butter, red grapes and string cheese, dried cherries and raw nuts, turkey jerky and a favorite fruit and go, go, go!
(COR-Condition Daily: Healthy Relationship with Food)

Week 16: Avoid eating after 7:30 P.M.
Our body doesn't need fuel to go to sleep and yet many people eat later in the evening. When you slowdown in the evening, emotions may begin to surface. Journaling (a mindfulness activity) is a great way to get in touch with the issues behind your emotional eating. So pick up a notebook and pen instead of a fork and write!
(COR-Condition Daily: Mindfulness)

Week 17: Eliminate carbonated and sugary drinks
Cola-based soft drinks have been linked to increased insulin resistance and inflammation in your body. Studies have shown that diet drinks actually increase hunger![vi]
(COR-Condition Daily: Healthy Relationship with Food)

Week 18: Add 10 more minutes to your walk and bump it up to 5x a week. You are now at 30 minutes for a total of 150 minutes a week! You did it!
If you don't have time to walk 30 minutes, split it up into 10 minute segments! Consider other forms of movement to vary your 150 minutes a week: line dancing, exercise DVDs, bicycling, golf, gardening. Make it fun!
(COR-Condition Daily: Movement and Play)

Week 19: Enjoy a 3-4 oz. portion of fish twice a week!
Hopefully, you are already eating some fish each week but this week let's make it a regular and conscious practice. Select seafood that is rich in omega-3 fatty acids such as salmon or trout. Tuna is another easy to prepare fish to add into your day.
(COR-Condition Daily: Healthy Relationship with Food)

Week 20: Unplug! Switch off the TV and other electronics during your meal. Eat slowly. Use all your senses and enjoy your meal.

Studies show that we consume more calories than we need if we eat while watching TV or playing a game on our phone. Unplug and listen to music or talk to family members, coworkers or friends during your meals.
(COR-Condition Daily: Healthy Relationship with Food)

If you have abided by these suggested changes over the few months, you should be feeling better emotionally and physically! You should be experiencing less cravings and feel that your addiction is better managed. Keep implementing these new behaviors in your life and stay on the path of more energy, better health and a healthy relationship with food!

---

[i] Nutrition and Healthy Eating. Water: How much should you drink every day? Mayo Clinic website
http://www.mayoclinic.org/healthy-living/nutrition-and-healthy-eating/in-depth/water/art-20044256

[ii] 23 and 1/2 hours: What is the single best thing we can do for our health?
https://www.youtube.com/watch?v=aUaInS6HIGo

Brain Science, A Miracle Cure for Willpower, McGonigal & Buczynski.
https://www.youtube.com/watch?v=gpk1kt2N5KI&noredirect=1

[iii] Whole Grains Council: What counts as a serving?
http://wholegrainscouncil.org/whole-grains-101/what-counts-as-a-serving

[iv] Vegetables and Fruits. Harvard School of Public Health Web site.
http://www.hsph.harvard.edu/nutritionsource/what-should-you-eat/vegetables-and-fruits/

[v]

[vi] Schulze MB, Manson JE, Ludwig DS, Colditz GA, Stampfer MJ, Willett WC. A review by the Journal of American Medical Association: sugar-sweetened beverages, weight gain, and incidence of type 2 diabetes in young and middle-aged women. JAMA. 2004;292(8):927-934.
C

My *Just One Thing* Tracker

Week:	H20	walk 10 min 3x	2 veg.	Am I Hungry?	2 fruit	3 whole grain	honor hunger	protein	eat min 3x	walk 20 min 4x	Add yellow veg	dairy 3x	tune in	prep veg/ add 1	fuel up	7:30	no soda	enviro	150 min!	Fish 2x per week	no inf	un-plug
1																						
2																						
3																						
4																						
5																						
6																						
7																						
8																						
9																						
10																						
11																						
12																						
13																						
14																						
15																						
16																						
17																						
18																						
19																						
20																						
21																						
22																						

Made in the USA
Las Vegas, NV
03 July 2024